WHO CARES

Is there a God who cares for you?

Susan McCaffery

Grosvenor House
Publishing Limited

This book is published by
Grosvenor House Publishing Ltd
Link House
140 The Broadway, Tolworth, Surrey, KT6 7HT.
www.grosvenorhousepublishing.co.uk

A CIP record for this book
is available from the British Library

ISBN 978-1-80381-700-2

Foreword

"Susan McCaffery often brings inspired exhortations to praise and worship, encouraging and challenging in equal measure. Her strong foundations in Jesus coupled with intercessory gifting enables her to point out where the UK is missing the mark, while earnestly praying for light, deliverance and breakthrough. Susan's other publications have proved to be valuable evangelism tools and have spread over England and beyond. "Who Cares" is a potent reminder that God's Shekinah glory isn't something we should presume on or take for granted and as Susan takes us through bible history, linking key events to the corresponding outpourings or paucity of God's glory, she reveals important meanings and warnings for us today."

– Worship leader of BEFC Peter Backwell

"Susan McCaffery's book is well put together and full of useful information, a good insight into God's Word. It's very encouraging to read."

– Theo Demson

Billericay Free Evangelical Church (member)

susmcCaffery@gmail.com

Contents

List of abbreviations from Bible references

Gen.	Genesis	Zech.	Zechariah
Ex.	Exodus	Mt.	Matthew
Chron.	Chronicles	Eph.	Ephesians
Is.	Isaiah	Tim.	Timothy
Jer.	Jeremiah	Gal.	Galatians
Ez.	Ezekiel	Rom.	Romans
Hos.	Hosea	Mk.	Mark
		Rev.	Revelations

Introduction to
"WHO CARES?"

The beginning of the year 2020 was different to any other we had experienced before in the UK, and in the world. Was there a virulent and dangerous virus about to break out into the world? The World Health Organisation, doctors, and scientists began warning of an imminent disease about to invade the planet. We were told immediate action must be taken to prevent the spread of this virus named Corona-19, so we must be shut in our houses and only go outside to get food, walk the dog, or for medical reasons. And when outside we would need to wear a mask.

So, I felt the Lord God said to me that as I had plenty of time on my hands, I could read some of the Christian books on my bookshelf that I had not looked at for some time: books on prayer, warfare, outreach, and so on. Spring moved on to summer. The restrictions were lifted, and it was a lovely warm summer, so I was able to get into the garden – weeding, trimming hedges and bushes, cutting the grass, and of course walking the dogs.

Autumn came and, with it, further restrictions. It seemed a variant of the virus had appeared, as dangerous as the first, so we were back into lockdown again. I don't often hear words from God, but sometimes get a thought which does not seem to come from my own mind. This time I felt the Lord say I should read some Christian books which I had not read before. From Clifford Hill, about a rebellious people, Israel, and now the UK, and the need to repent; Derek Prince on being a Prayer warrior; Rees Howells on Intercession; Smith Wigglesworth on Faith. Then the theme changed to something I'd not really considered before in any detail: Kynan Bridges mentioning the "Glory of God"; Colin Dye on "Glory in the Church"; back to Derek Prince about "God's Glory"; and Tommy Tenney the "Glory Chasers". John Bickersteth, with Timothy Pain, wrote the "Four Faces of God", and more recently I've come across "Do it again Lord" by Gordon Pettie, "Turnaround Decrees" by Jon and Jolene Hamill, and of course there were constant reference to the Bible – the New King James edition.

Outline of the book

In thinking about the contents of these books, which I believe God led me to read, then asking the Lord for inspiration, three booklets grew in quick succession. "The Good News" is a testimony of how the Lord has guided me since becoming a "real" Christian. "Where Did We Go Wrong?" covers how we as Christians and a church have moved far away from God. And "Reformation and the Church" looks at what Christians and the church have neglected and forgotten over the years – to truly know and experience the full, entirely powerful glory of God, His awesomeness, brilliance in appearance, and the mighty God who performs miracles. In the UK, we have lost – and indeed many have never experienced – the total magnificence of God, and we need to discover this again to fully empower Christians to reveal God to the world.

In this book I have tried to give you a flavour of what the Lord has shown me in the books I've read, especially in the Bible – God's inspired word to the world – together with the booklets that God inspired me to write. Outlining what I have experienced of God leading me over the 40 years since I first became a Christian, I have called this book "Who Cares?", with a subsidiary title: "Is there a God who cares for you?" It has not always been easy, sometimes wondering if God is there, if He is real. But looking back over the years, I realise the answer has to be yes. God is real, because I have met Him and heard from

Him. He has guided me in difficult times and healed me of sickness, led me to places I would not have thought to go, brought me to meet some amazing people, and on occasions given me a glimpse of His Glory. These things I would like to share with you to encourage you to seek more of God on your continued walk with Him, so you can have a greater experience of His Majesty, but even more, come to know His great love for you.

The book attempts to answer three questions. Firstly, "Is there a God who cares?", giving some answers to those who have doubts or who disbelieve. And this is shown through the life of one man, a family, then a nation, to whom God chose to reveal Himself, that He exists and has a purpose for him and all mankind. Secondly, "A God who cares for you," tells how God has shown in my life how he cares for me and can help you to know how much God cares for you. Thirdly, "How God cares for the people of world", highlights how the church began, and more specifically how the church grew in the UK. Finally, I try to answer the question "Where have we gone wrong?" and suggest how this might be put right. I used the term "church", because most people have an understanding of what is meant by that. But the word "church" really relates to the people, not a building.

I pray that as you read this book, it will inspire you and many others to also see the way forward for the church in the UK, that this nation will again become the people God intended us to be, reaching out to the people of the world with the love God has for us.

PART ONE
IS THERE A GOD WHO CARES?

CHAPTER ONE

Is there a God?

Some believe the world has been in existence for millions of years, beginning with a big bang. The question is what caused this bang? Did it come out of nothing? Surely something must have caused such a mighty explosion. It could not have come out of nothing unless caused by a greater being. But that would imply the pre-existence of a being who created this bang. Then again, where did the water come from with enough food in it to cause amoeba-like creatures to develop, and how could they grow into creatures able to come out of the water onto the land? You might then ask how the land appeared for the creatures to come onto it, with enough food to help them survive and procreate? Surely some kind of being must have caused these things to happen.

Eminent scholars have spent much time showing how the geological rock formations would have taken thousands, even billions, of years to come into being. How ice ages changed structures, wind, rain, and ice breaking down mountains, together with earthquakes and volcanoes, sea levels rising and falling, and changes of climate. Then after these tremendous surges of earth's terrain, creatures developed from an amoeba-type animal in the sea, grew legs, and were then able to come out of the sea and walk across land. Many and varied types of creatures emanated from the original creatures, until eventually they developed into an ape-like creature – one which over many years was able to develop its structure and skeleton until it could stand upright on two legs. And so, man appeared. I would suggest there needs to be a greater deal of faith in this thesis than to believe that a being had a hand in all this development!

There is another matter to consider in this evolution theory, where everything seemed to happen by chance. If creatures evolve, why are there no apparent discoveries of new creatures over the time that man has appeared on the earth? There may be development of new breeds of animal, but within the same animal category. A dog is always a dog, though there are many different breeds of dog. Similarly with cattle and horses. I would suggest there is a particular reason for this, but one which I will explain later.

Another matter to consider is about being accountable. If children are not accountable to their parents, they are likely to be disobedient and run wild, doing as they please, disregarding the needs of others, fighting to get their own way. Similarly with adults, if there is no accountability, we can easily run riot, disobeying rules made for the benefit of society, stealing possessions, and robbing people of food, money, or living accommodation. All matters which we hold dear in a civilised society.

But there is another view. The Bible describes how the world and the universe began rather differently. It begins with the affirmation that "In the beginning God created the heavens and the earth" (Genesis ch.1v1), and then says: "The earth was without form and void." (Gen. ch.1v2) What it does not say is how long the earth was like that! There are those who think it was a short period of time, but I wonder how long the "Spirit of God was hovering over the face of the waters". Perhaps it was years, even millions of years, in human time, though to God time does not exist. It is here for our benefit not God's. What is really important is the next verse. "Then God said, 'Let there be light', and there was light." (Gen. ch.1v3). Now you might begin to think, how real is this? To speak out a word and it comes into being, is that possible? Let us think more about how speaking out a command can make it happen.

There is a saying "sticks and stones can break my bones, but words can never hurt me!", and it's something children used to shout out at someone who used derogatory words towards them. But in fact, we can be hurt, angered, or made jealous by words said by another person. Now we even have a law about hate crime, based on what someone says about another. Accusations shouted out can undoubtedly hurt and have a powerful effect on a person. Words such as "you're too fat" or "you're skinny" can make young people feel ugly or unwanted. Christians are told to speak out in prayer and prophecy. Jesus has given us all authority to bind, cast out, pull down, or bless people and situations. This is what the role of the church should be, prophetically guiding the government and leaders in whatever capacity – in situations like poverty, sickness, even extremes of weather – by spoken words in prayer, intercession, and prophecy. Jesus said to Christians that we should go and tell others and make disciples of all nations. (Mark ch.28 v18 &19) To tell by speaking!

God's creation of the world continues with Him putting a firmament or expanse to divide the waters, so there is water below, in the earth, and water above, in the sky as clouds. In fact, until Noah's time there was no rain, only water springing up from the earth. The water above was in the form of thick cloud to protect humans from the harmful rays of the sun. It is thought the earth's temperature was kept at a constant temperature of 72F because of the thick cloud covering. The waters below were in the earth, coming to the surface in streams and rivers. But to begin with, the earth was completely covered in water. Then all the waters were gathered together in one place, so dry land appeared.

A few years ago, a computer study examined lowering the sea level from what it was at present to where it would have been before the flood which God later caused. Amazingly, the earth took the shape of a primula flower. The eye or centre of the flower was in the middle of the earth, and I believe that the centre was where Jerusalem is now situated.

Having dry land, God then created vegetation. After all, it would not have been helpful to create animals before food was there for them to eat. Now, there is a view that God created everything in one week, but I wonder if this was a human week or a God week? There needed to be plenty of vegetation for all the animals to eat regularly, which could take time. Then stars were put in the sky, together with the sun and the moon, so there was light during the day which helped the vegetation to grow. After that, the earth was ready for the first living creatures – fish in the waters, birds in the sky, and all kinds of living things which moved across land. The Bible says, "God created great sea creatures and everything that moves – according to their kind." That is according to their type of animal, not one type crossing over to another like cats with dogs or cows with chickens. Within each animal type there may be different breeds, but this cannot evolve into another type of animal.

Everything was then ready to prepare the way for Man to be created. There was the warmth of the sun and light by day, vegetation which could be used as food, and dry land on which to live. Man – the ultimate being God created, for His own delight, made in the image of God. So, He created

Man, who He called Adam, in His own image. How was that? God is Spirit, but He is a wondrous, magnificent, tremendous being, surrounded by a powerful, majestic splendour, covered in Shekinah glory. Adam, created as a human being but in God's image, was covered with this same Shekinah glory, with clothing like a bright, white light, his human body encompassed by God's glory, and His presence.

God put Adam in a garden, known as the Garden of Eden. There, he talked with God, and was aware of His Holiness, Majesty, and Sovereignty. Then God said He would create for Adam a friend, helpmate, and companion, who could share the Garden. While Adam was asleep, God took a rib from his side and made it into a woman. He brought her to Adam so that together they could share in God's glory and presence, and Adam called the woman Eve. Then God said, "Therefore man shall leave his father and mother and be joined to his wife, and they shall become one flesh." (Gen. ch.2v24)

Yet another being, called Satan, was already on the earth with his demonic angels. He had been banished from heaven, where he was known as Lucifer. He had been the leader of the worship, clothed in majestic beauty, leading angelic music in heaven, but he had desired to take over from God, and was immediately banished to earth. Jesus said, "I saw Satan fall like lightning from heaven." (Lk. 10v18) Satan was determined to get his own back by causing Adam to sin and be disobedient so that he could no longer experience the glorious times he had with God, meeting Him in the garden in the cool of the evening and talking with Him. (Gen. ch.3v8) Instead, Adam would be condemned to hell. So, Satan tempted Adam to eat the fruit of the tree God had said he was not to eat. Adam disobeyed God, and the Shekinah glory left him. Then he and Eve saw their nakedness and they immediately hid from God, but He found them and cast them out of the Garden of Eden for their disobedience.

However, God wanted to make a way for Adam and the humanity He had created to return to Him, and He had a plan! Sin caused Man to be disobedient and he became increasingly wicked (Gen. ch.6v5), rejecting God, having "constant evil thoughts in their heart". So, God had to flood the earth and destroy all humanity, except for Noah – a just man – and his family. (Gen. ch.6v9) From Noah and his three sons and daughters, humanity procreated and spread out, until they planned to build a city with a tower like a portal or opening, which would reach to heaven (Gen. ch.11v4), so they would be like God! Again, God had to intervene. This time He caused their languages to be so confused that they would not understand each other, then He scattered humanity across the face of the earth. (Gen. ch.11v8) But God still had a plan to bring humanity back to Him. And this time He was looking for a man who would be obedient to God's calling.

CHAPTER TWO

Who makes a covenant with one man and one nation

In a place called Ur, near where the River Tigris and Euphrates converge, was a man named Terah, who was the head of his family. The village was being invaded by another tribe which worshipped the moon god. Terah worshipped the sun god, and rather than be forced to change his allegiance, he decided to take his family north, between the two rivers, and go to the land of Canaan. When they arrived at Haran, though, Terah and his family settled and did not go any further. Terah died there. Who knows, if he had followed his first intention he might have received God's blessing.

When Terah died, his son Abram (later known as Abraham) became head of the family. And he was the man to whom God chose to reveal something of Himself. When Abram was seventy-five He was called by God to leave that country and go to a land which God would show him. God gave promises to Abram that He would make him father of a great nation and make his name great. Now, this all sounds really easy, but if Abram heard from God, he must already have had an acquaintance with Him, been aware of God's voice, and know that he could trust God to lead him to a new country. (Gen12v1)

If God calls you to do something, you'd better make sure first it is He who is calling! When I went to Bible School and joined with others on short-term missions, I began to realise this was a training ground for later. Then God encouraged me to go by myself on short-term missions to Uganda. When the Holy Spirit gave me a nudge and said, "You go," I knew it was God's calling or I could not have gone to a country I had never visited before and to a place where I only knew one person!

So, Abram became familiar with God's voice, as it says in Gen.ch 12v1, "The Lord SAID to Abram." But Abram did sometimes have doubts. God said he would be the father of a great nation, yet Abram did not as yet even have a son! So, God set about assuring him. He told Abram to collect a heifer, a female goat, and a three-year-old ram, along with a turtle dove and a young pigeon, to have as a sacrifice. They were to be cut in half and placed opposite each other, with a space between. Abram sat and watched, and as the sun was setting he fell into a deep sleep. It became very dark as Abram heard the voice of God telling him about his descendants. Then something like a smoking oven and a burning torch passed between the sacrificed pieces. "On that same day, God made a COVENANT with Abram, speaking many promises, revealing His Nature, Power and Authority." (Gen 15 v 17)

You might think this was a gruesome act, but in fact it was the custom of the time to confirm a marriage or alliance with a king, tribe, or any other matter of significance with this blood covenant. It showed a binding agreement, and if either one broke it, the one who broke the covenant would pay with the price of blood. Usually, the lesser one would walk between the divided pieces to confirm the covenant, but this time God Himself walked between them. This covenant will take an even more important place in the story of how God reconciled Himself with sinful humanity as we proceed.

So, God revealed Himself to this one man by saying, "I am the Lord who brought you out of Ur… to give you this land to inherit it." (Gen 15v7) This land was Canaan, the land God promised to Abram. Time passed, and when Abram was ninety-nine years old, God again appeared to Abram, saying He would make a covenant with Abram – a promise that he would be the father of many nations. His name would now be changed to Abraham, and his wife Sarai's name to Sarah, because the "h" indicated that the breath of God was within them.

Also, Sarah would be blessed with a son. Sarah laughed when she heard this, as she was ninety years old at the time. But God continued that the son's name would be Isaac, and that the covenant would continue to him and his descendants. As a sign of this covenant, God told Abraham to circumcise every male in the family and all the men in his household. A while later, Sarah became pregnant. Nothing is too difficult for God! When Sarah later died, Abraham purchased a plot of land there with a cave, in which he buried her. Let no-one dare say that this land, now called Israel, does not belong to Abraham's descendants!

I have written this in great detail to show how God went to vast lengths to begin to introduce Himself to humanity by revealing Himself to ONE man – Abraham. Similarly, with Abraham's son Isaac, when he became the head of the family, God renewed the promise He had made to Abraham. The Lord said, "I am the God of your father Abraham, …I will bless you and multiply your descendants for my servant Abraham's sake." (Gen 26v24) Isaac had two sons (hardly a great nation!) and God chose the younger, Jacob, to continue the family line. Even though he was a cheat and a liar, he had a spirit which God could use to draw him closer to God.

He revealed Himself to Jacob when he was running away from his brother, whom he had cheated. Jacob rested in a place later called Bethel, near to Jerusalem, and there God revealed Himself to Jacob in a vision, where he saw a portal with angels going up and down a stairway. Then he heard God's voice saying, "I am the Lord God of Abraham, your grandfather and of your father Isaac. The land on which you lie I will give to you and your descendants." (Gen 28v13) Then God assured Jacob that He would be with him and not leave him. God once again revealed Himself with a covenant to one person.

COVENANT WITH HIS FAMILY

Much later in Jacob's life, after many trials, God changed Jacob from a lying cheat to a man of humility before God. You might think that the nature and personality you are born with is permanent. But with God that does not have to be so. As you draw near to Him, He can change your attitude, personality, and temperament from one who cheats, lies, and is jealous and angry with everything, to a kind, considerate, loving, and compassionate human being – if you ask Him. One night, as Jacob was scheming and planning how to placate his brother whom he had deceived many years earlier, he found himself alone with a Man, God's Angel, who wrestled with him all night. Jacob was determined not to let go until, now humbled, he had received a blessing. Jacob's thigh joint was dislocated in the wrestling, and he walked with a limp for the rest of his life. But this whole event changed Jacob's attitude completely. He was now suitable to continue the line of descendants from Abraham, with his name changed by God from Jacob (deceiver) to Israel (contender with God).

During his lifetime, he fathered twelve sons, who all kept covenant with God by being circumcised. The tribe began to grow in number, but they were a nomadic family, spreading out across the land. God wanted them to become more united, and He had a plan! It began with one of Jacob's youngest born, called Joseph. He was a proud whipper-snapper of a boy, and he had some wonderful dreams of his father and brothers bowing down to him, which caused his older brothers to become very angry with him. They planned to kill him, but the eldest brother Reuben persuaded them to sell him as a slave to passing traders, who took him to Egypt to sell him. (Gen 37)

God's plan didn't seem to be working yet in the eyes of man, but wait! Joseph was thrown into jail because his integrity caused him to escape from the advances of the slave owner's wife. Sometime later, the Pharaoh had a dream of seven fat cows grazing and then being eaten by seven thin cows, but they remained thin. Joseph, through God, was able to interpret the dream – that it showed there would be seven years of plenty followed by seven years of famine. As a reward, Pharaoh made Joseph head of his government to deal with the coming severe famine.

Joseph had made sure there was plenty of food stored in Egypt, but famine was also in Canaan. The brothers had to go to Egypt, where they were reunited with their brother, Joseph. His father, renamed Israel, was invited to Egypt with the rest of the family and they settled there. The family had now grown to seventy, in covenant with God, through circumcision. They remained there for four hundred years (Gen. ch.42-50), rearing sheep and cattle, and growing prosperous because God blessed them. Their numbers grew to thousands, but though they were separate from the Egyptians, they became increasingly under the power and authority of the Egyptians. God was looking for this Israelite tribe to grow into a nation, but they were too comfortable in Egypt.

God had a plan! A new Pharaoh came to power, who did not know about how Joseph had rescued Egypt at the time of the severe famine. He saw how this tribe of Israelites had grown in considerable number and was afraid that they would become even more numerous than the Egyptians and take control of the land. So, he decided to have all the newborn baby Israelite boys killed. However, the plan did not work too well, especially when a baby was born to an Israelite couple. He was such a beautiful baby that the mother decided to hide him in some bulrushes by the river. It so happened (!) that the daughter of the Pharaoh found him and decided to adopt him.

He was given the name of Moses, grew up in the Egyptian court, was treated as an Egyptian and learned all the ways of the Egyptian court. But he always knew he was part of the Israelite family. When he grew into manhood, he went to see his true brethren and saw how badly they were being treated. They were made slaves, and forced to work hard, making bricks. One day he saw an Egyptian badly beating one of the Israelites and was so angry that he killed the Egyptian. He was soon found out and had to escape or be killed himself. (Ex. ch.2 v15)

God's plans do not always seem to work at first, but let us progress further. Moses fled to Midian. As he was sitting down by a well, the daughters of Reuel – the priest of Midian – came to water their flock, as they had been chased away by some shepherds. Moses protected them so they could water their flock and return home early, and as a result Reuel invited Moses to come and stay in his house. He even gave Moses his daughter Zipporah to be Moses' wife. They had a son who they named Gershom, meaning stranger, for Moses said he was a stranger in a foreign land. Nevertheless, he settled into his new family and spent his time looking after a flock of sheep as a way of earning a living. He had arrived there at the age of forty and was now nearing the age of eighty.

Meanwhile, back in Egypt, the Israelites were suffering terribly in their slavery and began to call out to God for help. (As an aside, when will the UK begin to call out to God for help in their present situation?) God remembered His covenant with Abraham, Isaac, and Jacob, and He had a plan! One day while Moses was leading the flock of sheep, he happened to see a burning bush. This was not so unusual. In the heat of semi-arid land, bushes occasionally burst into flames, but what was so unusual about this bush was it did not burn into ashes but continued to burn brightly. So, Moses went closer to inspect it and got the fright of his life when he heard a voice say, "Moses, Moses, take your sandals off your feet, for the place where you stand is holy ground." The voice continued, "I am the God of your father, the God of Abraham, the God of Isaac, and the God of Jacob." Moses was very afraid.

Just imagine you are walking along, thinking of nothing in particular, and this voice burst into your thoughts and introduces Himself as God. Have you ever had a similar experience? Has anyone you know become so aware of God's presence that they are filled with fear? I believe not. The UK has gone so far from God that many even deny His existence. But God is near; He is waiting for us to call out to Him; He has a plan!

God gave Moses his instructions. He was to return to Egypt, go to Pharaoh and say, "God says, 'Let My people go, for them to return to the land I have promised to Abraham.'" Can you imagine how Moses felt at the enormity of what God was telling him to do? Moses' first response was, "No, I cannot do that. Why me?" But because he had spent his childhood in the Pharoah's palace, he was the ideal person to go to Pharaoh, knowing the ways of the Egyptians.

Moses began to ask God a number of questions. Can you begin to imagine the audacity to argue with God, who he had probably not considered greatly, nor ever had a deep conversation with before? "Who shall I say sent me?" asks Moses. God assures Moses He will be with Him and tells him to go with the Israelite Elders to the Pharaoh and ask Pharaoh to let the Israelites go into the wilderness for three days to worship and give sacrifices to their God. "What if they will not believe me?" Moses asks. God shows Moses a miracle using his shepherd's staff, which he is told to throw on the ground, where it changes into a snake. Then he is told to pick it up, and it turns back to a shepherd's staff. God said he could use this staff to perform miracles. But Moses still protests, saying he is not eloquent of speech. God tells him to take Aaron, his brother, to speak for him. On his way back to Egypt, he is reminded that in returning to the Israelites he first needs to circumcise himself and his son to reconnect with God's covenant with Abraham.

THE PLAGUES

God knew Pharoah would not easily agree to let the Israelites go. Something would have to occur to make him change his mind. So, God brought forth ten plagues, all connected with the gods the Egyptians worshipped. Each one was more terrifying than the last. God told Moses to use his staff in front of Pharoah and turn it into a snake. The magicians there were able to do the same, but Moses' snake ate up all the other snakes!

Other plagues appeared each time Moses went back to Pharaoh demanding that the Israelites be allowed to go, and was refused. The waters of the River Nile became as blood; a plagues of frogs came out of the river; then a plague of lice; a fourth plague was of thick swarms of flies; then a severe pestilence on all the Egyptian cattle, including horses, donkeys, and camels, killing them all – but not those of the Israelites. Still Pharoah would not agree to let the Israelites go, but God reassured Moses that Pharoah would agree in the end.

You might wonder why all these plagues are being identified. Having written about God's power, this is demonstrating just how powerful He was, and I've not finished yet. The last plague was something much greater. The sixth plague was of boils, and the magicians were unable to perform something similar. The seventh plague was devastating hail all across Egypt, but not where the Israelites lived; the eighth a plague of locusts, demolishing all the crops in the land; and the ninth a plague of such darkness that no-one could see throughout Egypt, except where the Israelites lived.

PREPARATION FOR THEIR PASSOVER

Before the tenth plague, God prepared the Israelites with specific instructions. On the tenth day of the month, each Israelite household was to take a lamb, without blemish, and prepare it for sacrifice. The Elders were to sacrifice the lambs on the 14th day. It was to be called the Passover lamb, because the blood of the lamb was to be sprinkled on the lintel and the two door posts. All the inhabitants of each house were told to stay indoors until morning. That night "the Lord will pass through to strike the Egyptians and when He sees the blood on the lintel and on the door, the Lord will pass over the door and not allow the destroyer to come into your houses." (Ex. ch.12v23) This final plague – the death of every first born Egyptian – included Pharoah's own first born.

Why was this sacrifice necessary, you might ask. It was meant as a means of repentance for sins committed. God told Abraham to sacrifice his son, to test his obedience. When Abraham showed he was willing to do even that, God relented, and Abraham saw a ram caught in a thicket and sacrificed that to God instead. What is interesting, however, was that while taking his son to the mountain where the sacrifice was to take place, Isaac – Abraham's son – asked where the sacrifice was. Abraham answered that God would provide the sacrifice. This proved to be correct. God did provide the sacrifice, but as we shall see later, it proved prophetic again some two thousand years later.

God ordained this to be called the "Passover", to be remembered each year to ensure that this and the other miracles showing God's power and desire to have the Israelites released from captivity, would never be forgotten. But it had a greater significance than that. God said the life was in the blood and they were always to drain the blood from the animal before cooking and eating it. This blood, however, was for a different purpose. It was to indicate that Israelites were inside the house, and not to be harmed. This blood was therefore for protection, and would have an even greater significance later.

Finally, Pharaoh told them to go, and as they were led by Moses to the Red Sea, the whole Israelite family was protected by God. Then Pharaoh changed his mind and sent the Egyptian army to chase after them. The Israelites crossed the Red Sea, because God parted the waters by a miracle and led them towards the promised land. The Egyptian army chasing after them were drowned on entering the Red Sea because God let the water return.

The Israelites entered Egypt as a family of seventy, and four hundred years later left Egypt with over one million people – husbands, wives, and children. God was keeping His promise to Abraham that he would be the father of a great nation that would populate the world. But now they had to become united as a people and a nation. This would take time. God gradually revealed a little more of Himself and His character, able and willing to perform many mighty, powerful miracles. God showed His faithfulness in keeping His promises to be with Moses and give him the words when he spoke to Pharaoh. He also now revealed His Name. When Moses said, "Who shall I say has sent me?" God replied, "I am who I am. Say 'I am' has sent me to you." (Ex 3v14)

So, Moses next led the Israelites from the Red Sea into the wilderness of Shur, where they encountered their first problem – there was no water. As they moved on, they came to some water which was so bitter that it could not be drunk, and the people began to complain. It was the first of many tests, for God was showing them to listen to Him and keep His commandments, and they would be free from problems and diseases. God said, "I am the Lord who heals you." (Ex 15v26) And all the time, the descendants of Abraham's family kept the sign of their covenant with God by the boys being circumcised as babies.

CHAPTER THREE

Who reveals his Shekinah glory

The Israelites wandered on for three months in the wilderness, complaining when there was no food, then that they had no meat, and each time God provided. He sent Manna – a kind of sweet tasting wafer bread – in the mornings, and quail as meat in the evenings. When they came to Mount Sinai, they camped, and Moses went up the mountain to talk with God. How wonderful that Moses seemed to have direct communication with God. Are we so fortunate today?

Then God revealed more of His plan to Moses. He said that the Israelites were to listen to His voice and keep His covenant so they would be a kingdom of priests and a holy nation. Moses went back to tell this to the people, who readily agreed. They were to sanctify themselves, ready to meet with God on the third day. God was to come to them in a thick cloud and speak to them from the cloud, so they would all hear Him speak to Moses but not go up the mountain.

Can you imagine the excitement, yet fear, of coming to meet with God? A trumpet was to sound to draw the people near to the mountain. There was smoke like that of a furnace, the mountain quaking, and a long trumpet blast getting louder and louder, as Moses spoke to God and God answered him. (Ex 19) Then God called Moses and Aaron to come to Him up the mountain, where He gave them the Ten Commandments. (Ex 20) These are the Commandments which God intended to be for all people, so that they would worship and obey God and know how to treat other people. God gave Moses many more commands and instructions while he was up the mountain, enlarging on His original Ten Commandments. This included the command to keep the Sabbath as a day of rest, as an additional sign of their covenant with God.

Below, the Israelites were probably confused and fearful, wondering what was going to happen next. Moses, their leader, was on top of a mountain where fire was raging. He was away so long that they wondered if perhaps he had died. What should they do while waiting? Singing, dancing, children playing. Was God there? What about worship, and praising? After all, in Egypt there were many gods to worship, so perhaps they should have one – like a golden calf? This was all so new to the Israelites who had lived in Egypt for many generations. Even now they were not really used to trusting and having faith in something they could not see, so why not build a calf idol and call that their god?

When Moses came back down the mountain, he was shocked and became very angry at what he saw. The Israelites were dancing and singing around a golden calf. A feast had been proclaimed, people bringing offerings, eating and drinking around an altar which Aaron had built, and saying that the calf was their god who brought them out of Egypt.

Are we any better today? Worshipping other gods such as Mammon, the god of money, material goods, exotic holidays, pop concerts, sex, and celebrating? The Israelites were "unrestrained"; are we today? Moses threw the tablets with the Ten Commandments on them, written by God, onto the ground. (Ex. ch.32v19) He destroyed the idol and had those involved killed. Later, when God told Moses to again go up the mountain, He renewed the covenant by giving Moses instructions to write down all that He was telling him and to tell the Elders.

God also said they would be to Him a kingdom of priests and a holy nation. This was to be no ordinary promise; it was to have greater implications for the Israelites than perhaps they realised at the time. They agreed to obey all that God had told them to do, (Ex. ch.19v8) knowing God promised that He would do marvellous and awesome things. But He warned them to observe the covenant and not make a covenant with the other inhabitants of the land which God was to help them take. (Ex. ch.34v10-12). The covenant which was written down became known as the "Book of the Covenant".

THE TABERNACLE

While the Israelites were wondering in the wilderness, being led by a pillar of cloud by day and a pillar of fire by night, God wanted then to be more aware of His presence and know that He was always with them. So, He instructed Moses to build a moveable structure where His presence would reside. He called this structure a Tabernacle. It would be a remarkable tent, suitable as a place in which God's presence could be experienced. People were asked to bring offerings with which to build the Tabernacle, and of course they had plenty to bring, because the Egyptians were so anxious to see them go that they gave them everything – gold, silver, jewels, garments, linen, and beautiful material in splendid colours. He also gave specific instructions about the measurements of the structure, the colours of roof covering, the curtains and decorative features to surround the Tabernacle, the artefacts, containers for sacrifices, lighting, anointing oil, the altar, and the fire. (Ex. ch.36)

Words cannot sufficiently describe the colours of the linen white curtains embroidered with blue, purple, and red thread, and the gold of the artefacts – the splendour and magnificence of the Tabernacle when it was completed. Each colour had a particular significance. The gold to represent God in His glory; the blue representing the sky and heaven; the off-white of the linen, the sinful man; purple to signify royalty; and the red, the blood shed in sacrifice to receive forgiveness for the people's sins. These were the colours also wrapped over and on top of the Tabernacle; the red signifying the blood especially to show for protection of the Tabernacle and the people.

Within the Tabernacle was to be a box, called an Ark, in which was placed God's Testimony of the Ten Commandments in the "Book of the Covenant", Aaron's staff which had budded when the other elders' had not, and a pot of manna that had been preserved. On top of the Ark was a seat, called the Mercy Seat, with Cherubim above this – all made of acacia wood but covered with gold. It was put in a curtained-off section called the Holy of Holies, where God would meet with Moses and speak with him from above the Mercy Seat (Ex 25v22) about things concerning the Israelites.

In the Holy Place, outside the Holy of Holies, was the golden lampstand with six branches, three either side and a main one, filled with oil to give permanent light. Specific instructions were given about the altar for sacrifices and the other artefacts. This was God's design for the Israelites.

It was to be a meeting place where they could experience God's presence, His awesome beauty in the colours that they could see, and to be a place where they could praise and worship the God of Abraham, Isaac, and Jacob in the splendour of His glorious presence. "When the Tabernacle was complete and fully erected, a cloud covered the Tabernacle, and the Glory of the Lord filled it." (Ex 40v34) So powerful was the glory that Moses could not enter.

TOWARD THE PROMISED LAND

The twelve tribes of the Israelites made their way toward the land which God had promised them. Twelve men, one from each tribe, were told to go into the land to spy it out, see what it was like, report back, and bring some fruit too. The spies found it was indeed a land flowing with milk and honey, and they brought back some beautiful, fine fruit. But they had found a problem – the land was full of giants! It would be impossible to defeat them, so they said not to go into the land. Only two disagreed – Caleb and Joshua – even though Moses reminded them how God had enabled them to escape Egypt and protected them from the chasing Egyptian army, even providing a way of escape by opening the Red Sea for them to cross.

So, the Israelites refused to go forward. They forgot how God had shown His power and might to them against Pharaoh and revealed Himself in the wilderness by having a glorious Tabernacle built where His Presence resided as they travelled and rested. They were not yet ready to trust God to help them overcome their enemies and protect them on entering the Promised Land. Though they had seen and experienced so much of God's might, they rebelled against Him, and He had to keep them wandering in the wilderness until they had sufficient faith and trust in God that they would willingly go forward.

When Moses died, God spoke to Joshua, who had been Moses' assistant, telling him to take the whole Israelite nation over the Jordan into the Covenanted Promised Land. This happened to be at the time of the spring rains, which meant the river Jordan was in full flood. God chose this moment to again demonstrate His power and glory. The Ark, now called "the Ark of the Covenant" because it contained the "Book of the Covenant", was first carried to the water's edge by the priests. Immediately, the flow of water stopped, a miracle held it back upstream, and the Israelites all crossed over on dry land.

Their next obstacle was a city called Jericho, which would have to be conquered to enable the Israelites to make their way through the Promised Land. Then the "Commander of the Lord's Army" (Jesus, before His time on earth as a human being) appeared to Joshua and gave him instructions about how to attack and defeat the people of Jericho. This was not by fighting with weapons of war, but by marching around the thick walls of Jericho once each day for six days in silence, on the seventh day to march around seven times in silence, and then for the priests to blow their trumpets and the people to shout "a great shout". Over a million people all shouting loudly must have been a huge noise! And the walls fell down! This was no mean feat, as the walls were so thick that people had their houses in the walls. God was again showing His power and might, and it must have been an awesome sight!

Before they had crossed the River Jordan, God had told Joshua to always obey the Book of the Law (which God had inspired Moses to write). Now, in the battle against Jericho, God's instructions were to take nothing.

Cattle, valuables, women, everything was to be destroyed so they would not be contaminated by things which were cursed. However, some were greedy and took valuable gold and silver ornaments for themselves instead of dedicating them to God. So, when the next city (Ai) to attack was nearby, everyone was confident that as this was a small place it would be easily defeated, and they enthusiastically decided to attack it. But the men of Ai fought back, a number of Israelites were killed, the army was defeated and ran away. Distraught, Joshua pleaded with God, asking why He had not helped them. God replied that there had been sin and disobedience; someone had stolen the valuables which were meant to be presented to God.

Joshua continued leading the Israelites into the Promised Land, gaining territory as they went. The king of Jerusalem called other local kings to come and fight against the Israelite army by first fighting against Gibeon which had made peace with Joshua. God told Joshua not to fear for He would deliver the Israelite army, but it took more than a day, and Joshua asked the Lord to extend the day until the battle was won. Who would have thought it, to have the sun and moon stand still for twenty-four hours, but this is what God did. For He created all things and had control of all things.

I once heard of two men carrying out an experiment to see how far back the computer would go in years, and what would happen when they arrived at year zero. One man gave an exclamation just as a scientist who was a Christian was passing the door. The man had noticed as the dates reversed over 3,000 years that one day was missing. "Oh," said the Christian, "that was when Joshua asked God to extend the day for twenty-four hours." (Joshua 10)

JUDGES AND KINGS

Not all of the Promised Land was conquered, though. Joshua died, and there was then no real leader. The generations which had known God, His mighty deeds, and his awesome power, had also died. And without this experience, the Israelites began to sin and do evil in God's sight. (Judges 2v11) In time, after Joshua, God began to raise up leaders called Judges, who advised the people, but there were still wars, rebellions against Him, and a lack of knowledge and understanding of who God was, His power and authority, awesomeness, and holiness, or any real sense of worshipping their great and mighty God.

So, we move on in the history of Israel to a time when, at the people's request, God raised up Kings. Samuel, the then High Priest and Judge, was told by God that He had identified Saul as king. But he was a failure, being disobedient to God. Next God chose a young lad called David. He did not immediately become king but learned to trust God because Saul, in his jealousy, tried to kill him but David was protected by God. By then, the Israelites had conquered some of the Promised Land and settled down in their tribal areas as God had indicated to them. There were often skirmishes and battles against other tribes, but God decided it was time that a permanent place was built in which His presence would reside. He gave David instructions about the measurements of this building, the contents, and utensils. A part was to be sectioned off, called the Inner Sanctuary, with a huge, thick curtain behind which would be the Ark of the Covenant, and the Mercy Seat with Cherubim above. It would be such a holy place that only the chosen priest would be allowed to enter it once a year, just as it was with the original Tabernacle in the wilderness. But this was to be a glorious Temple where the people would meet to repent of their sins, come before a Holy, Omnipotent God, and worship Him.

THE TEMPLE IS BUILT

God told David that as he had been involved in many battles, he was not to build the Temple but put the Ark in a Tabernacle which David erected in Jerusalem. David then sang a song of thanksgiving in which he said they were to remember the covenant which God had made with Abraham. Instructions were given that his son Solomon was to build the Temple when he became King. And this is what Solomon did at the beginning of his reign. (1Kings ch.6) No stone blocks were to be fashioned at the site, it was to be such a holy place. Huge vessels and containers were made of bronze; bronze oxen to support these vessels with ornamental buds and lily blossom around them; capitals with ornamental pomegranates; panels engraved with Cherubim, lions, and palm trees; the altar, furnishings, and lamp standards all covered in gold. Then finally the Ark was brought into the Temple and placed behind the curtain in the Inner Sanctuary.

When the Temple was completed, Solomon called all of Israel to a great dedication. There was much celebration, sacrificing of animals, worship, and praise to God. Finally, Solomon dedicated the Temple to God. (2 Chron. ch 6v12) It was a magnificent prayer, suitable for the occasion, and God responded in a mighty way: "Now when Solomon had finished praying, fire came down from heaven, and consumed the burnt offerings and the sacrifices; and the Glory of the Lord filled the Temple. And the priests could not enter the house of the Lord because the glory of the Lord had filled the Lord's house." (2 Chron. ch.7v1&2)

And the people of Israel bowed their faces to the ground and worshipped the Lord.

INTO EXILE

You might think by now that the people of Israel had enough understanding of who God was, His attributes, love for them, and desire to lead them to peace by worship and being obedient to His laws. But the sins and pride of the people led them to continued disobedience. After Solomon died, there were disagreements among his sons. The nation became divided into two – known as Judah and Israel. Israel was led by its kings into more and greater idolatry, rebellion and rejection of God as their leader and guide, worshipping the gods of the local tribes. And there came a time when Israel was completely overrun and dominated by the stronger nations from the Assyrians to the Babylonians.

The nation of Judah survived longer because they had a number of obedient kings who led the people back to God, but eventually they too were overrun, and many were deported to Babylon. Yet God had not finished revealing Himself. During these years, He appeared to a number of prophets, each time revealing more of His character, His power and almighty magnificence, but warning of what would happen if the people of

Judah rejected Him. Even when they deported to Babylon, God raised up a number of prophets. Isaiah had a vision of God sitting on a throne, high and lifted up, and His train filling the Temple. (Is.6v 1) He was surrounded by seraphim, crying to each other, "Holy, holy, holy is the Lord of hosts; the whole earth is full of His glory." (Is. 6v1-3) God was helping Isaiah see something of heaven, its magnificent, splendour of colours, with awesome seraphim surrounding His throne, and beautiful harmonious singing in praise of God.

Later, God spoke to Isaiah about an extension of His covenant, saying that He would keep Judah (Israel) "and give you as a Covenant to the people as a light to the Gentiles". (Is 42v6) This is God revealing His purpose for His chosen race. In time, they were to reveal to the world the nature and desire of God to be known by all people, so they would understand how they could be forgiven their sins. Yet, in spite of these wonderful promises, God's people began to wander away from Him. They accepted the idol worship of other nations and adopted their practices, and God had to raise up prophets to warn them. Isaiah said they would be punished for their disobedience, but a new king called Cyrus would enable them to return. (Is. ch.45v1) Jeremiah said God was rebuking them and reminding them if they did not keep to His covenant they would be cursed. (Jer. ch.11v3) And again later, "the men who have transgressed My Covenant will be given into the hands of their enemies." (Jer. 34v17-20)

Most of the nation was taken into exile, and though the Ark was lost, God still kept close to them, revealing Himself to Daniel. He was one of those sent into exile but was close to God and received visions and prophetic interpretations for Nebuchadnezzar, and later Belshazzar – the kings of Babylon. Then he had a vision for himself, of God, who he called "the ancient of days, whose garment was white as snow, His throne was a fiery flame, wheels a burning fire and thousands ministered to Him". Then, as Daniel was watching, "One like the Son of man (Jesus before He came to earth in human form) came from the clouds of heaven to the Ancient of Days, to whom was given dominion and glory and a kingdom." (Daniel ch.7v9-14) He also saw four hideous beasts: one was destroyed and given to the burning flame; the others had their dominion taken away but their lives prolonged.

Up till now, we have seen God's power and might. Here we see something more awesome yet sinister, and the prophecy for Daniel was not just about the present but the future of the world! But that is another story.

When Daniel read from the Prophet Jeremiah that their stay in Babylon would be for seventy years, he began to pray by first confessing that God was a great and awesome God who keeps His covenant with those who love Him and keep His Commandments. He began to pray that God would, in fact, keep to this promise. It was not just an ordinary prayer, though. He began to fast, wearing sackcloth and throwing ashes on his head, as was the custom. Neither were his prayers just about the Israelites returning to Jerusalem. No, it was a much more profound, serious prayer, lasting over twenty days. He confessed the sins of the people, who had committed iniquity, done wickedly, and rebelled against His Commandments. He talked of the shame they had for sinning against God, who is Righteous, pleading to Him who is merciful and forgiving to hear these prayers. (Daniel ch.9v3-19) Did God answer Daniel's prayers? Of course. He is a faithful God who had made a covenant with Abraham that he would be the father of a great nation. This was God helping that nation to return to Him in obedience, worshipping and praising their God.

Ezekiel had a vision of God, described as "a whirlwind from the north and a great cloud with raging fire, the brightness of an amber colour out of the midst of the fire, with wheels beside each living creature. Then from the fire came four living creatures, each with four faces. One face was like a man, the second like a lion, the third an ox, and the fourth an eagle, with wings which touched each other, and their appearance was like burning coals of bright fire, and lightning out of the fire." (Ez. ch.1v4-16) Each time God reveals His glory, it seems greater and more magnificent than the last. Can you hear the sound of the whirlwind, the crackling of the raging fire, and the wheels moving with the creatures?

THE FOUR FACES

So, what is the relevance of the four faces to God's glory and the revelation of Himself to the world? Think of Jacob who had twelve sons. The sons had families who grew into tribes, and as the Israelites went into the wilderness, God told Moses to camp together in these tribes. There were four senior tribes – one to be in the centre of three tribes as they camped around the Tabernacle. Each tribe had its own emblem on a flag or banner. Judah's emblem was a lion; Joseph's an ox; Reuben's a man; and Dan's an eagle. These emblems, spoken by Jacob to his sons – with God's inspiration – gave prophetic insight into their natures. (Gen. 49v3-28) But what is the meaning of these four faces in Ezekiel's vision?

How do they relate to the rest of the Bible? We can see the answer to this, particularly when we look at the Gospels. The lion is called king of the beasts; Jesus is called King of Kings. The Wise Men came to Jesus when He was born a human being, with gifts of gold, indicating He was a king. So with His resurrection, Jesus showed He is King over all kings and Lord over all lords. He will return to earth to rule as supreme King. The ox is known as a beast of burden, a servant to man. Jesus took our burdens upon Himself at the Cross and was a servant to all. Reuben, a sinful man, but Jesus the perfect man, became the perfect sacrifice. Dan's emblem of an eagle reflected Jesus the divine spiritual eagle. So, Jesus was not just God-born as man who lived a normal human life. There was more to come.

Ezekiel also had his vision of the Temple in Jerusalem, while he was exiled in Babylon. Later, Ezekiel in ch10 describes the Glory of God as he saw it in all its magnificence and splendour, having first seen the evil, the bloodshed, and the abomination in the Temple (Ez. ch.9). And he says in verse 18, "Then the glory of the Lord departed from the threshold of the Temple." Yet God still had a plan for this nation to be able to reveal Himself to the world.

RETURN OF THE ISRAELITES

A new king came to the dominant kingdom, named Cyrus. (Is. ch.45v1) He proclaimed that, "He (God) has commanded me to build Him a house at Jerusalem, which is in Judah." Cyrus continued, "Anyone who wishes to return back to Jerusalem may do so." (v4) God inspired many to return and take with them silver, gold, goods, livestock, and the articles which Nebuchadnezzar had taken from the temple built by Solomon. Hundreds went, but many also stayed in a place which they found it comfortable, because Jeremiah had earlier told them to build houses and settle down in Babylon.

Whether they left Babylon or stayed, there had been a number of changes over the seventy years the Jews had been in exile. It was as if God wanted them to change their lifestyles to be prepared for the next stage in their development as His chosen nation. He intended the Jews to later reveal Him to the world as a loving Father, merciful and righteous, who was faithful in keeping His promises, but who required people to be obedient to His laws for the benefit of all mankind. When they first went into exile, of course, there was no temple in which to worship God, yet this was instinctively what they wanted to do. Being in a strange place, they still needed to be able to do something which was familiar to hold onto God. Their desire was to still worship God, their comforter and helper, and they began to see this could still be done without the Temple, but in their homes and small buildings called Synagogues.

Zechariah, another prophet, spoke words of encouragement, saying God would restore Judah and Israel, that Judah would be delivered from exile, and the idols' names would be cut off, so God's Covenant would be restored. But they would "look on Me whom they have pierced; and will mourn for Him." (Zech. ch.12 v10) This seems to be full of contradictions, and its entire meaning would not become clear for many years.

PART TWO
A GOD WHO CARES FOR YOU

CHAPTER FOUR

Coming to know God

How did I come to know all this? Let us go back forty years. As I neared my 39th birthday, I moved to Billericay in Essex and settled down while continuing my career in teaching. It was the house the Lord found for me, with front and back rooms, a large garden, well established but ready for improvement. But soon something began to niggle me. I had a good job, a nice house and garden, but it did not seem to be enough. Perhaps there was more to life than this, I thought, but what? For months I wandered around with that question in my mind, not finding the answer.

Have you ever felt like that? Asked yourself what am I here for? Do I have a purpose? If so, what is it? How do I find it?

One Sunday in March 1980, I drove to Walton-on-the-Naze, walked in tears along the rock-strewn beach, turned and began walking up the hill close to the cliff top, still thinking there must be more to life. There were thick brambles protruding onto the path, and peeking out from them a plinth. Written on it was Psalm 66, verse 4: "All the people of the earth shall worship You, they sing praise to You, they sing praise to Your name." A tall figure stood in front of me, His arms outstretched. I just knew He was Jesus, and somehow I knew the answer to my question, but I could not have explained how and why then. It took me months to piece together why Jesus was the answer. Gradually, Jesus helped me to become more at peace with myself.

JESUS CAN MAKE A DIFFERENCE

But how was it possible for Jesus to make such a difference in my life? After all, don't we spend much of our time getting on with life without Him? Well, you can try, but when problems and difficulties come into your life, when you are made redundant, are seriously ill, physically or mentally, have relationship problems, or someone close to you dies, how do you overcome the fear, anger, jealousy, or hatred that wells up inside? Firstly, because He loves all those He created – that is you and me – and wants to help. But secondly, and more importantly, He made it possible to help us overcome life's difficulties because He took upon Himself all our burdens. You see, the anger, hatred, fear, jealousy and so on are usually against our fellow man or woman. This is called sin, and it usually causes us to then become unhappy with ourselves and even ill, which is where I was when I began to look for the "what more is there to life?".

The good news is that Jesus overcame all our sins by His sacrifice of Himself, being crucified, dying on the cross that we might be saved from our sin. The Bible explains all this. If you believe this is possible and have faith to accept that Jesus can take from us all the dross in our lives, then we have to ask Him to come into our lives, to take away our sins, and make us clean and fresh with a new life. Why not do that now? Ask Jesus to give you faith to believe He can and wants to help you. Tell Him you are sorry for all the times you have rejected or ignored Him. That you want to change, to have a new life and way of behaving, to be free from fear, anger, jealousy, hatred, and instead know his love, compassion, mercy, and forgiveness. GO ON, DO IT NOW! Talk to Him, but be careful what you promise. God may take you at your word!

Perhaps you think Jesus would never appear to you like that. He can still become real to you, but you have to work at it. Firstly, try to begin reading the Bible, because Jesus mostly speaks to us through His word, which He inspired 40 people to write down over 1,500 years. The word Bible means library of books, because that is what the Bible is. It has a total of 66 books – 39 in what is called the Old Testament, and 27 in the New Testament. Don't try to read it all at once. Begin with one of the Gospels – like Mark's gospel – and use a modern-day translation like the NIV (New International Version) or NKJ (New King James). What is even more interesting is that Jesus can also talk to you through the Bible. Words and phrases can jump out at you in such a way that you can come to know Him in a closer way.

Another thing which will help you through is this. I began my search when I was so unhappy with life that I tried to find out what was missing. When you realise that Jesus is the missing part, first you come to realise how you have neglected or rejected Him and need to say how sorry you are for that. Then ask Him to help you. Find a church which will baptise you fully in water, then ask the Holy Spirit to come and teach you about Jesus and His way of living. When I prayed that the Holy Spirit would come into my life, being prayed for by the minister at the altar rail, I was filled with such joy that I could not stop laughing for some time. Then it became easier to read the Bible with greater understanding.

CHAPTER FIVE

Jesus loves me

I read that God loves me with an everlasting love (Jeremiah ch.31v3), and came to experience it in a wonderful way. I was walking along the beach in Felixstowe one November afternoon as the sun was setting. The clouds above were grey, as you would expect on a late autumn day, and the sea seemed to reflect the same grey colour. Suddenly, looking toward the distant horizon, a break appeared between the sky and the sea, and the sun peeked through in a beautiful rose colour which spread across the clouds and was reflected down onto the sea. It gave such a glorious pink hue across the whole horizon that I realised even on a dull November day, the beauty of God's creation could be seen across the whole of Felixstowe. And not only that. God had given me eyes to see and appreciate such a glorious sight. I had such a wonderful feeling of love for Jesus, who could give me such an insight into His glory that I began dancing along the promenade singing "I'm in love with Jesus!"

It also says in the Bible that Jesus was God on earth in human form and He knew me before I was born. (Psalm 139v13) There was a time when I shared with a Christian that I thought I was a mistake. The Second World War had begun, and I thought my parents were looking for solace rather than bringing a baby into the world at such a time. The Christian said we are never a mistake; He knows us even before we are born. It is at the right time and for a purpose. As we come to know Jesus more, we will find our purpose in this life. He placed me on this earth at this time for a special reason (Psalm 139v16), to draw others to Him. (Mt 28v19) Do you have a strong desire to know what more there is to life? Keep seeking until you also find the answer. Don't give up. Keep searching until Jesus gives you the answer. For I found in reading Psalm 23 that Jesus is my Shepherd and Guide, my Protector, Comforter, and Provider, who leads me in the way of righteousness.

There may be times, too, when you actually hear God's voice. Some find this is often the case. I have to confess this has only happened to me infrequently, but I could not doubt it was God speaking to me. One instance was when I was quite a new Christian, standing in a group of more mature Christians in prayer. One of the group began to speak in tongues. No-one knew what she was saying, but her husband prepared himself and I thought he was going to give us the interpretation. He took a little while to begin speaking, and my mind began to wander until a loud voice bellowed in my ear, "This is for you, listen!" I almost jumped to attention as I began to listen most carefully to what was said.

Another time, when walking toward Snowdon mountain in Wales, I missed the right path near the top and found I was following a sheep track which disappeared. In looking around, I heard a shout, "Scree!" In geological terms that means there is danger from loose soil and stones, likely to cause a landslide. I made my way carefully down the one hundred feet or so to a path below and asked the climbers there if anyone had called out. The answer was in the negative. God had warned me! On a third occasion, feeling rather depressed and even wondering if God did exist, I stood by the seashore on a beach in Felixstowe and said aloud, "Are You there, God?" Beside me was a seagull which suddenly took off, and as it did, I heard the words, "I am in the sea, the sky, and in this seagull." Oh, I thought, You *are* listening!

Soon after I'd become a "real" Christian, I said to God that I'd continue teaching until I was 55 then work for Him. (The cheek of it!) Some fifteen years later (don't think God always moves quickly!), having joined the choir at church, been baptised in the Holy Spirit, then led by Jesus to move to a Pentecostal church, I found I had M.E. – an illness that makes your body become tired and painful after a little exertion. It was difficult to think, remember, concentrate, and function as a normal human being. I had to retire as a teacher, but then I asked the Lord if He wanted me to remain as a cabbage for the rest of my life. The answer came as I read the latest Pentecostal magazine. I looked at a blank page with a small square in the centre with tiny writing on it and thought it was stupid. I turned over the page then was curious and wondered what the tiny writing said. So I turned back the page. It talked of a Bible School, and I felt compelled to enquire about it. Having explained at the interview that I could not think, write, or communicate, because I was ill, I was reassured that it would be alright because they would pray for me.

BIBLE SCHOOL

Many days during the first term, as I struggled through London in the rush hour, I was almost collapsing on arriving at Kensington Temple, where the Bible School was being held. But every time, students came round me, praying that the Lord would heal me. It was not just any "ordinary" Bible School. Lectures were often interspersed by the lecturer saying, "Let us pray about this." And we began most mornings with prayer, praise, and inviting the Holy Spirit to be with us. Often there were practical sessions with prophetic words being spoken over students and opportunities to preach. Gradually it became a little easier. The Lord was answering prayers for healing, and after attending the courses for two years, I believed I was well enough to take part in the Mission course, which was not just theoretical but practical. At some point I realised that I was 55! God had taken me at my word.

This led to short-term missions with other students, and we went to places such as Sao Paulo, where there were many miracles, and I experienced the great power of the Holy Spirit when there was preaching and ministry. Then to Belfast, at the time of "The Troubles". It was a surprise to see armed soldiers standing on guard along the streets, and I felt a little fearful until one soldier called out with a cheery voice, "Hello."

When in Belfast I realised how God uses anyone, even little me, for His purpose. I have an Irish surname but was born in England. And suddenly I felt a deep conviction of having to say to the prayer meeting we were attending that the English in me was having to ask forgiveness of the Irish in me for how the English had treated the Irish in the past. I was in tears and found it difficult to speak the words, as I was so overcome, but two weeks later the peace accord was begun. There had been many people praying, politicians discussing and negotiating, but it seemed that Jesus used me in part to set up the peace accord. You may think that God would never use you in this or any other way, but there may be a time when you are used in a large or small way to change situations, if you are obedient.

MY MISSION STATEMENT

Having received my diploma from the International Bible Institute of London (IBIOL), I felt Jesus was encouraging me to continue with mission to "Go out and make disciples". In reading Isaiah 40, verse 31 spoke to me as if the Holy Spirit was encouraging me to go on "wings like eagles". It was a kind of mission statement; my purpose or calling. Do you believe you have a calling, that Jesus has a purpose for your life? It may not yet be apparent but ask Him to show you.

In looking back over my life, I could see how Jesus had prepared me for that time. Before becoming a Christian, during many years there was a prayer which I often prayed. "Lord Jesus, may I see You more clearly, Love You more dearly, and follow You more nearly day by day." It took Jesus twenty years to answer that prayer, and then another ten years of healing of life's hurts before I learned about the Holy Spirit and how He strengthens and enables us to do the work He calls us to do.

CHAPTER SIX

Mission to Uganda

I found myself going on short-term missions to Uganda during a period of around twelve years. Do you believe nothing like this could ever happen to you?

One Sunday, sometime after I'd received my Diploma from the Bible School and was waiting for God to move, a Ugandan Elder came to my church and asked if anyone would like to come to Uganda, as they would be most welcome. The Holy Spirit gave me a nudge and said, "You go." So I did! I went on my own but in the strength of Jesus, and over a period of twelve years I visited on short-term missions of two or three weeks at a time. The second year I was there, I said to God, "What am I doing here?" In conversation, I was told the number of churches was growing but Pastors could not afford to go to Bible School. Back home, I found that Colin Dye – the senior Pastor at the Bible School I attended – was putting all the information and teaching into book form. So, the idea "came to me", from the Holy Spirit, to take these books (twelve of them) to Uganda and teach the material to the new Pastors there, three books at a time.

The titles of these books were a little unusual. No boring theology or church history. Instead, they were about knowing the Father, the Son, and the Holy Spirit. Others were entitled

"Worship", "Effective Prayer", and "Glory in the Church". It was wonderful to see how hungry everyone was to hear about God's Word. Prayers followed with healings, deliverance, and praise to God for His mercy. You see, being a Christian is not just giving your life to Jesus; that is only the beginning. Hearing God speak to us, often by reading the Bible, means we have to learn what the Bible is about. Most of us need healing, physically or emotionally, to see why we should forgive, help others, and find the gifts God has given to us to help others. This information is all in the Bible.

There were a number of events I particularly remember during my visits to Uganda that showed God was leading the way and protecting me. One year, as soon as I arrived at my base with Pastor Jane, she announced, "We are in a drought!" I found this hard to believe as there were so many banana trees with their large green leaves, as well as other trees and a lot of grass. But I asked if they had prayed about the problem and the answer was in the negative. So, the next day, as I was driven to a small church in the bush and after much praise, worship, and prayer, I encouraged the congregation to pray for rain. This was not something I often did, however there was a great deal of energetic, enthusiastic praying and then I began the journey home. Looking around, I was disappointed to see the roads completely dry until… wait a minute… was that a small damp patch on the road? And another? And larger patches? By the time we arrived back at base, there were thick clouds, thunder and lightning, and the rain poured down for at least an hour.

Another time after praise, worship, and preaching about the church on a hill being the light to shine all around – as this church was on the top of a hill – I felt the Holy Spirit whisper to tell them He wanted to heal eyes.

Not having experienced such healing before, I gulped at this, but nevertheless I announced what the Holy Spirit wanted to do. There were many cheers and at least half the congregation of nearly two hundred came forward for prayer. Then I was whisked off to another church to preach, and it was only three years later when I returned to that church that I found out if any had been healed. A woman came to me saying her eyes had been healed at that time, but they were getting weaker again so she asked if I would pray for her.

There was a time when I was driven to a prison to speak to the inmates. The room was filled with about three hundred men, one guard with a very rusty looking gun, me, with two Pastors. Inspired by the Holy Spirit, what I said was well received, and almost all the prisoners stood up when asked if they would give their lives to Jesus. But the enemy was not happy! As we travelled back down a narrow winding road, we drove into thick smoke where banks of grass were burning. The driver suddenly could not see and, at risk of crashing, we had to call out to Jesus to help us.

On a third occasion, the car was confiscated by the police! The policeman pulled us over to the side of the road, walked suspiciously around the car a number of times, then gleefully pointed at the road tax which was out of date. We had to go to the Magistrates' Court, which happened to be nearby, and were forced to pay a large fine. The driver was also threatened with prison, even though he was not the owner of the vehicle. Prisons in Uganda are rather different to those in the UK. For example, food had to be provided by relatives, the cells were sparse, and there was no nice cuddly prison warder to tuck you up at night! No-one had enough money to pay the fine, but we couldn't let the driver go to prison. So, what were we to do? The owner had to be contacted.

To my surprise, the Magistrate kindly let us go to phone the owner, who happened to be the President of this group of churches. But we needed to find a phone. Mobile phones were available at kiosks, so two of us walked to the nearest kiosk, while I was praying all the time that God would make a way. No reply. We went to report back to the Magistrate, but I stayed outside, still praying! The Magistrate even allowed us to try phoning again, but with the same result. On the way back to the court the second time, my Pastor friend had a good idea – no doubt inspired by God – to offer to leave the car as collateral, instead of paying a fine. And the Magistrate agreed. I'm not sure he was always so kind to Christians, but I think God answered our prayers!

On arriving in Uganda late one year, I went to my room and settled down for the night only to be awakened by great cheering, singing, and sounds of instruments. On enquiring the next morning about the cheering, I was told that the church had overcome the enemy. The witch doctors had caused problems and some Christians had been thrown into prison, but after a great deal of prayer, this decision had been reversed. The Christians were released and the witch doctors were put in prison instead. However, that was not the end of the matter.

I heard during that year that the President had died, and an Elder had invited another Pastor to join the leadership. But he was of a different spirit, and the whole community of nearly one hundred churches was in danger of splitting up. After much prayer the matter was resolved, but when I returned the next year, I felt the Holy Spirit inspire me to say they had forgotten to shut the back door. Spiritually, the witch doctors had got their revenge because the Pastors had neglected to seek a protective covering from God.

Chapter Seven

How Jesus helps
us overcome difficulties

Have you experienced situations in your life which are difficult, painful to contemplate, or just made you feel you are useless and of no consequence? Look to see how Jesus is allowing this, to give you experiences that can be used to help others to His glory. This leads on to my experiences of how Jesus released me from past sins of not acknowledging Him as God and Lord of my life, of having a childhood where love was not emphasised. I was born at the beginning of the Second World War, with enemy aircraft flying overhead and dropping their bombs onto Kent if they had not successfully hit their London targets. Air raid warnings and dashing into next door's shelter were common. So, I had a childhood of experiencing fear and where love was difficult for parents to express because there was no real security, without God.

It seemed a good idea for me to learn more about Christian Counselling, so I could help other new Christians to be released from all the cares and worries which we pick up through life. It's funny to think about it now, because although I did not realise it at the time, my need to be released from many burdens was God's first priority! As I arrived, a lady came out of the room next to mine and said, "Oh good. I prayed that I would find a friend, and here you are!" That began a friendship of many years. And even though at first we did not know each other, she became my Mentor.

We met on a number of occasions, and as we lived one hundred and fifty miles apart, our meetings were very special. We talked and prayed, read scriptures, then talked and prayed some more. Gradually my hurts and fears, feelings of uselessness and no purpose in life began to change, until one time I became filled with a deep sense of Jesus' love for me.

There was a time when someone close to me died, and I was distraught for months. At church someone talked about a Pregnancy Crisis Centre being set up. Thinking I had experienced bereavement, which many who have had abortions also experience, it seemed good to help and I applied to train as a counsellor. During the course Jesus helped me to first overcome my own sadness, learning how the client is taken through "The Journey". It would begin with where the client was at: angry with herself and jealous of others who were pushing prams or carrying babies; full of remorse at what she had done, never able to forgive herself. Or in some cases, having closed her mind to the event until sometime later she became mentally or physically ill and sought help to relieve her of the anguish. With the guidance of the Holy Spirit, gradually the client was brought to know Jesus and that He does not condemn but always wants to heal mind, body, soul, and spirit.

The client can be led to the moment when, realising she needs to repent, she can ask Jesus for forgiveness and becomes aware of His love. This leads to the client being healed of the negative thoughts and physical sickness. There is no forcing the client to go any further than she wants. Sometimes repentance is too difficult, but there are usually one or two Christians in the background praying that the Holy Spirit will help to make a way.

On becoming qualified, I looked with anticipation to counsel my first client but I never seemed to have any. God, however, had other ideas. Instead of being a counsellor, I joined the Trustees of the Centre and eventually became the Chairman, using skills I had picked up during my years as a Deputy Head Teacher.

You may find that Jesus leads you in a different direction to me. No two individuals are the same in character or experience. Sometimes, even as Christians, we can experience depression or jealousy, guilt or hatred. If you are unable to forgive yourself or another person, Jesus might help you to work through these problems on your own, with His help, but often He brings you alongside another or a small group who can listen, to pray and ask Jesus for direction. Other difficulties might be encountered with the enemy who does not want you to be released from all the baggage that surrounds us through life. Remember, even Jesus was tempted when He was led into the wilderness by the Holy Spirit. (Luke ch.4 verse 1-13) His answer each time was to remind Satan of what the scripture said. This is the best way to overcome temptations of any kind, but first of all, you do need to read your Bible to let God speak to you through His inspiring Word. What is important is to know that Jesus loves and protects you. His shed blood was a final sacrifice to enable our sins to be forgiven and protect us from the enemy. Ps. 91 is a good one to read and pray about if there seems to be an attack from Satan.

Some will find this task daunting, feel shy or lacking in confidence, not bold enough to begin Jesus' commission.

First Jesus needs to help you overcome these fears by healing you and restoring you to be the person He created. When we are baptised in water, Jesus' Spirit enters our spirit and awakens it. We learn that He redeemed our lives by giving His life as a sacrifice for our sin of rebellion, so He is our wonderful Saviour, enabling us to receive eternal life. But that is not all! Jesus also said as He was preparing to return to His Father, that the disciples were to remain in Jerusalem "until you are endued with power from on high". (Luke ch.24v49) If you want to be a dynamic Christian, full of power and discernment, with God's wisdom and prophetic knowledge, water baptism is not enough. You need the baptism of the Holy Spirit, too.

PART THREE
A GOD WHO CARES FOR THE WORLD

God did not intend to reveal Himself only to the Jews, but to the people of the whole world whom He created, so that all people could be reconciled to Him. As He was preparing to return to His Father in heaven, Jesus said that we were to go and make disciples of all nations, telling them of what God had done and why. This became known as the "Gospel message". When people believed the message, as an outward sign they were to be baptised in the name of the Father, Son, and Holy Spirit. Then He gives us all the authority His Father had given Him, to tell the gospel message to all nations.

Instead of sitting in huddles after the service, having a cup of tea and saying what a nice service it was, Jesus' command was to go and tell others that Jesus is alive!

CHAPTER EIGHT

Jesus comes into the world

For four hundred years after the remnant returned to the Promised Land, God was silent. There were no warnings about keeping to God's Laws or being loyal to Him. But they still worshipped God and read the Torah – mostly found in the Old Testament section of the Bible – remembering God's promise that He would love them and protect them, and even more importantly would send a Messiah who would reign over them.

This was particularly important when the Romans conquered the land, putting them under occupation with very strict rules, being charged taxes and severely punished if any Roman Laws were disobeyed. So they looked forward with hope that this Messiah would come soon, reign as King, and defeat the Romans. A new Temple was later built in Jerusalem by King Herod, who had been appointed by the Romans. A large building, made by human hands, it was for the glory of King Herod rather than God.

As we look at the beginning of Luke's version of the Gospel, in the New Testament, we read of shepherds on the hills near a place called Bethlehem, close to Jerusalem. They had probably just finished eating supper, having made sure the sheep were safe, and were thinking of settling down for the night, sorting out who would take the first watch, getting bedding ready, and perhaps looking up at the dark night sky covered with many twinkling stars. It was a still evening, quiet except for the occasional bleating of a sheep. Then suddenly, this peaceful scene was shattered by a bright piercing light stretching and covering the whole sky. There was a tremendous sound of thousands of voices singing in beautiful harmony, accompanied by trumpets, cymbals, drums, stringed instruments, and the Glory of the Lord shining all around them. Witnessing such a gigantic noise, with light so brilliant that the shepherds were blinded and deafened, they jumped up preparing to run away, until they heard a voice of an angel saying, "Do not be afraid, tonight is good news of great joy because the Saviour of the world, Christ, the Messiah, has come." Then, with the angel, the shepherds saw and heard multitudes of the heavenly host praising God and saying, "Glory to God in the highest, and on earth peace and goodwill toward men."

Jesus was a perfect, sinless being on earth. He taught a great deal on how to treat one other, get on with each other and love each other. To love our neighbour as ourself, regard each other with respect, and forgive not criticise each other. But He was also the perfect sacrifice and was crucified that our sins would then be forgiven when we repented. Jesus was the final sacrifice. Only He was acceptable to God the Father, and we should be forever grateful that Jesus was prepared to suffer excruciating pain and to shed blood that we might be forgiven and set free from sin. So, the New Testament gives us hope of forgiveness and eternal life. But more than that, God sent His Son, because He loves us and there was no other way to save us. Jesus came to redeem us and be our Saviour, because God created us from the womb to have a special part to play in the world and in eternity.

need to be aware of the enemy and know how to deal with it. But let us look at what happened after Jesus returned to His Father, in heaven.

In the book of Acts, we read about how the church began. The disciples were waiting in Jerusalem, in an upper room – as Jesus had told them to do – when suddenly, on the day of Pentecost, there came a sound from heaven, like the rushing of a violent wind, filling the whole house in which they were sitting. And there appeared to them tongues, resembling fire, which separated on each one of them. They were all filled with the Holy Spirit, and began speaking in other tongues, as the Spirit gave them utterance. (Acts ch.2v2-4). It was not the building that experienced God's glory but the people in it! Today the church is looked upon as the building, but Paul talks of US AS THE CHURCH, being part of Christ's body. (Eph. ch.4v12). It is the institutional church which has to understand this; it needs revelation and healing.

On that wonderful day of Pentecost, which the Jews still celebrate as Passover, imagine being in the Upper Room with 120 other disciples. Waiting there, in expectation as Jesus had told them to, in prayer, when suddenly the most marvellous, exhilarating, stupendous thing happened. The excitement was such in Jerusalem that when Peter explained that God had visited them in the form of the Holy Spirit, soon 3,000 others joined them. However, as they were all getting comfortable with this new life, God had to allow something tragic to happen which would cause these numerous disciples to move out of Jerusalem – just as Jesus had told them to do. "Go and make disciples of all nations." (Mt. ch.28v19) The Roman army completely desecrated Jerusalem, and everyone had to escape or be killed. But in fleeing, many found themselves in places where they could tell people about Jesus, His death, and His resurrection.

Different disciples who had known Jesus – called Apostles – began teaching about Him, His teaching, that we should love God and each other, Parables about the Kingdom of Heaven, preaching, showing how the Torah (God-inspired Jewish writings) had prophesied the coming of Jesus, the Messiah. They performed many healings and miracles, as the Holy Spirit was with them. And gradually the number of disciples, who became known as Christians, increased across much of the known world – Asia, Europe, and Africa. Soon the word was even brought to Britain!

CHAPTER NINE

Growth of the church

To overcome the sin that had entered the world, causing Man to no longer have a close relationship with God, He had originally begun His quest to redeem the situation by first revealing Himself to one man, then to his family, and then to the nation which it became. Now it was time for that nation to reveal God to the world! So, Peter – one of Jesus' closest disciples, began to speak, explaining what had happened. This is what was spoken by the prophet Joel. "In the last days, God says, 'I will pour out my Spirit on all flesh.'" It was the beginning of God reaching out into the whole world.

In the four Gospels you can find many examples of Jesus' teaching and miracles, then in the Acts of the Apostles, the beginning of the church. followed by much teaching about God and how we should relate to Him and to each other. This is all because God wants us to know about and experience His presence and His glory.

But being sinful human beings, it did not go well! There were objections and people were enraged at the thought that there was one true God above all other gods. Christians were thrown into prison for their beliefs, and even killed. But still the church grew in number. They had faith and belief in the true word of God and the Bible.

Today, many Christians are still being thrown out of their homes and villages and being martyred. That is why it is important to know what the Bible says about God, and in reading, praying, and worshipping to grow in faith and trust in Jesus.

During the nearly 2,000 years that the British Isles has had a Christian presence, there have been many ups and downs. It seems that there are times of Holy Spirit inspiration, when people give their lives to Jesus and accept the Christian culture of developing loving relationships with Jesus and with friends. Keeping the Ten Commandments, caring for the poor, speaking the truth, being honourable in work, and at home. Then gradually all this fades. Christians become comfortable in their situation and forget to continue telling the next generation the story of Jesus who came to draw us back to God. So, the power of God in their lives diminishes. Christians forget to reach out to God, even reject Him, and the power and glory ceases to be.

There are certain high points in history (His story) where the Light of Jesus shone brightly. From the Romans coming to Britain and telling the Good News to the English, and St Patrick taking the message to Ireland; in the 5th century, St. Augustine of Canterbury and other missionaries preaching the word to Scotland and Wales; til the Anglo-Saxons, who were pagans, fought against the Christians, – though later they were converted. From them came Alfred the Great, who was King of the Anglo-Saxons. He wrote the Doomsday Book of law, much of which was based on the Bible and until recently was the basis of many of the British laws. Then a time of darkness came over the land. But men were inspired to live in monasteries and keep writing copies of the Bible, so the word stayed alive.

There was a great revolution when the printing press was introduced into England by William Caxton, in 1476, because William Tyndale then translated the Bible from Latin to English, and had it printed. This gave Christians a wonderful opportunity to have access to the Bible and read it. In Europe, Martin Luther became concerned that to raise money for the building of the Basilica in Rome, the Pope introduced the idea that salvation and eternal life could be purchased through indulgences. Martin Luther read Romans Ch. 6v23: "The gift of God is eternal life." And he protested that this gift was not to be bequeathed by the Pope, but by God – a free gift!

Martin Luther was excommunicated, but because of him a group came out of the Roman Catholic Church and set up what became known as the Protestant Church. Why am I telling you all this? Because we have the established Protestant church in the UK, following a religion based on prayer books or forms of service which have gradually moved away from worshipping the God of Glory to worshipping the church, regardless of God.

Henry VIII had his own reasons for wanting to break away from the Roman Church, principally so he could divorce his wife Catherine of Aragon. This meant the church in England became Protestant (protesting against the rule of Popes over England). By the middle of the 1700s, Christianity was again at a low ebb, and God raised up a man to bring back revival again through the Holy Spirit. His name was George Whitfield. Born in 1714, he lived until 1770, spending much of his Christian life preaching with the inspiration of the Holy Spirit and drawing many crowds of people who responded to the message of Jesus as Saviour. John Wesley followed with similar inspiration and responses, and he spent many years riding around the country on horseback. It was a time of great revival, with churches becoming full under a new Methodism denomination – at a time when there was the awful demonic revolution in France. God saved Britain from that!

Trade was developing among many nations, and the slave trade became a way to get labourers, transport them elsewhere, and make them work. It is well known that Africans were transported across the Atlantic and sold as slaves to those owning sugar plantations in America and the West Indies. This was done by a number of European countries such as Spain, Portugal, and Britain. What is not so well known, however, is that Arabs and African Chiefs were also involved in selling African slaves, and on some occasions British people from Cornwall were taken as slaves, too. William Wilberforce, a Christian born in 1759, became convinced that slavery was wrong. Paul talks in Rom. 6 of being set free from the slavery of sin. And in Gal. ch.4v7 Paul says, "you are no longer a slave but a son". Wilberforce was a Member of Parliament and spent thirty years trying to get an Act passed which would make slavery illegal. He finally succeeded in 1791, and the Navy was then ordered to stop slavery wherever it was found. There were many battles, but gradually this was enforced.

The Holy Spirit again caused revival to break out in the middle of the 19th century, during Queen Victoria's reign. The industrial revolution had increased trade worldwide, but at the beginning of the 19th century there was much poverty in Britain. Another move of the Holy Spirit became so powerful that thousands were aroused, caused to repent, seek God for mercy, and be filled with a Holy Spirit baptism. It happened not only in this country; missionaries were "sent" to many parts of the world. On one of my visits to Uganda, I was told that the Chief of Buganda, part of what is now called Uganda, had sent a message to Queen Victoria asking her to send him Bibles!

In 1865 General Booth, a Methodist preacher, was so appalled at the poverty and drunkenness of the population in London and the many orphans there, that he set up "The Christian Mission", which he renamed the "Salvation Army" in 1878. He preached powerfully with the empowerment of the Holy Spirit, about needing Jesus as Saviour, giving those in poverty hope. He also wrote a book called *England and the Way Out*, and had homes built for the homeless, fallen women, and released prisoners. Many people were so touched by this that they contributed generously.

But the Holy Spirit had not yet finished. Around the same time, there were spasmodic revivals in Ireland and Wales. Then, as the 20th century began, came another move of the Holy Spirit. From Azusa Street in America to Wales, then other countries such as England, there came a mighty move of God. Some people were filled and empowered by the Holy Spirit, firstly to receive visions of God or be called to pray sometimes for hours and days. As they received fresh anointings and had greater experiences of God's presence, they were so convicted of their sinfulness that they repented deeply, sought and pleaded for God's forgiveness. From that they received a Holy Spirit baptism, becoming powerful in their preaching and evangelism, calling all to repent as the Holy Spirit fell upon the meetings.

Evan Roberts was one such minister, and he was so touched by God that he spent hours praying, repenting, and seeking forgiveness, then preaching so powerfully under the anointing of the Holy Spirit that thousands came to give their lives to the Lord. Coal miners came out of the pits and went straight to church because they so wanted to experience the power of God. The Police had no-one to arrest, and Magistrates' courts closed because there were no criminals to prosecute – such was the overwhelming power of God in parts of Wales at that time.

Smith Wigglesworth – in the late 1800s – and the Jefferson brothers were involved in the Pentecostal movement whose legacy has lasted until today. Selwyn Hughes and David Hathaway's fathers, through the Jeffersons' ministry, were filled with the Holy Spirit. And later, Reinhardt Bonnke, as a young man already filled with the Holy Spirit, was further inspired when meeting George Jeffreys. These are all people who have continued to influence us today through their preaching and ministry. However, revivals such of these never seem to last. Preachers become tired and worn out, disagreements take place between different denominations, and gradually the power of the Holy Spirit fades.

Chapter Ten

The church today

Since the end of the Second World War, there has been a great deal of social change and new technologies invented. The motor car gradually took more prominence with people travelling greater distances as family incomes increased. People were able to work further away from home, so less time was spent with the family. Women felt a new freedom; some mothers even began to go out to work while their children were still young. They became known as "latch key" children, getting home before their parents and lacking the warmth of a greeting and hug when they arrived home.

With the love emphasis in the 1960s, a new freedom began to include "free sex" for the older teenagers, resulting in unwanted pregnancies and backstreet abortions. A law was then passed in 1967 to make abortions legal for a limited number of pregnancies, to prevent serious problems with the backstreet operations. But gradually the abortion limit was extended, until today it is permitted up to twenty-four weeks of pregnancy.

God, however, was still active in drawing people to Him. The revival in the Hebrides around 1954 was the result of two elderly ladies praying for many years that the Holy Spirit would come. In the '60s, teens and young people were drawn to share the love of Jesus, and Billy Graham held evangelistic meetings where many responded to the call to give their lives to Jesus. Churches were happy to continue with Christian work among their followers, with Sunday worship meetings and Sunday School for the children, maybe a Bible Study during the week, and perhaps a Prayer Meeting.

In other ways church members had been very busy with open doors for Baby and Toddlers Groups, Pre-School, and Junior children's groups, as well as meetings for young teens and group gatherings for older teens. However, gradually there were less children attending and congregations became smaller. More recently, other forms of outreach into the community were developed. Lunchtime cafes for all-comers, sing-alongs for the elderly, and board games in groups for the more adventurous senior citizens. Some churches have instead reached out into the community to meet the growing needs of people, establishing food banks and some clothing banks. In a number of towns Christians have become Street Pastors, perhaps being aware of issues in the towns during the day; some living near railway stations are "Railway Pastors", to try and prevent the suicides which often occur in these places. There are others who help with debt advice, and a number of Christians are involved in Schools Ministries as Schools Pastors or Pregnancy Crisis Centres.

But this does not mean churches are necessarily increasing the numbers in their congregations, and I wonder why this is.

WHERE DID WE GO WRONG?

It was all going so well! Enough work, income, socialising, sport, eating out, holidays. Why has it suddenly all come to an end? Have we spent too much time enjoying ourselves, becoming flabby emotionally, not having to face many challenges, or struggling to survive? Like the Laodicean church mentioned by Jesus in Rev. ch.3 v15, are we neither hot nor cold and Jesus is ready to spit us out? What has been happening behind the scenes? Social media has expanded greatly, giving news and information that exaggerates – even falsifying the truth. There are more hurtful accusations and aggressive comments within society. Gone is the love, appreciation, and encouragement of earlier times.

Then the pandemic came. We have difficulty seeing through the false information we receive to what is the real truth. Is the virus causing many more deaths than in a usual winter? Is the vaccination really going to be effective? Will these "shutdowns" eventually come to an end, and people have the opportunity to return to work? Then a question not many seem to be asking is: "What is God doing in all this?" If He loves us, why does He not get rid of the virus so we can return to living our lives normally, in peace and health?

But let's look at the world as it is today. Some rich nations; others in poverty. Trafficking and slave trading for sexual purposes. An internet full of porn and gambling "opportunities", family break-ups, many single parents struggling to make ends meet, the homeless and those who rely on food banks, even in the UK. What is the world coming to, and where will it end? Do we deserve to "have it so good" when we in the Western world have used much of the resources such as oil, wood, land for building, to the detriment of the "third world" living in poverty, while we take all the fish from the sea, purchase quantities of food and throw much away while poor people starve? Then we produce so much plastic that the earth and the sea is being overwhelmed by it all.

Is it possible that God, if He exists, has said "enough is enough"? "I created a world full of beauty, sun to warm by day and rain that the crops might grow. The beauty of flowers and vegetation, with eyes to see. Birds with beautiful songs, and we with ears to hear and appreciate them, and you are trashing it all!" Is this how we want the world to continue? Our lives on hold, little work, low income, so we spend all our days struggling, with little money and bills to pay? Or is there a better way? Can we of the church make a difference?

LOOKING BACK

The letter of James in the New Testament talks of FAITH, but says that without WORKS faith is dead. (James ch.2v14) He means that we need to demonstrate our faith with good works, like events in the church building or being involved with people outside the church building. Yet there must be more! Why did God spend much time revealing His Glory in the Old Testament if it was not meant to continue into the New Testament and beyond, up to the present day? Is it because we often neglect the Spiritual side of our being, which God wants to touch as we worship, praise, and pray? Let us look back to what I have described earlier from the Old Testament

The Israelites may have had some excuse for not knowing God in His fullness, but we in the UK have no such excuse. We have been a nation which knew and worshipped the God of Abraham, Isaac, and Jacob for well over one thousand years. Magnificent churches and cathedrals have been built in which to meet, praise, and worship God, although these places soon degenerated into places of religious acts, instead of the worship of Jesus. But those who built the beautiful, imposing structures did so with the honest intention of building them to God's glory.

Words cannot sufficiently describe the colours of the linen white curtains, embroidered with blue, purple, and red thread, and the gold of the artefacts - the splendour and magnificence of the Tabernacle when it was completed, to give us a great vision of His Glory. And you can imagine my exclamation of surprise and wonder when, walking with my dogs along a path one warm spring morning, I went into a meadow and there were the same colours of blue in the forget me-nots, the gold of the buttercups, the white of the daisies, the purple of the, and red of the scabies. God had painted the same colours here as in His Tabernacle many years ago! His Glory was to be seen in that meadow!

Are our church buildings today such beautiful, splendid places in which to experience God's presence? Do we treat our buildings today with the same reverence as the Israelites in the Tabernacle which, when erected, was covered by a cloud and the Glory of the Lord filling it with such power that Moses was not able to enter? Oh, that today we would seek God's Glory and presence with such earnestness, we would cry out to Him with a desperation, pleading for God to come, waiting until He answers. Lord, how we need You at this time. Lord we plead for Your mercy. We are desperate for You to come and heal the institutional church and our sin-drenched land. Yet what do we mean by "the church"?

WHAT DO WE MEAN BY THE CHURCH?

Many look upon the church building as the answer. We "go to church"; meet other Christians in "the church"; worship God with hymns and songs in "the church"; and attend services in "the church". Then often we go home and get on with our lives. Of course, it is good to meet other Christians together, often inside a building because the weather is not always suitable in the UK to meet outside. But the church needs to be more than this. We are all part of the body of the church, but do we bring Jesus with us, in our spirits, praise and worship our Lord and Saviour, pray and invite the Holy Spirit to come with God's Shekinah Glory, into the meeting? This is where we can collectively meet and experience the power of God and commune with Him, in tongues, interpreting prophetic words. Speak words of encouragement to each other and exalt His Holy Name. Look to experience something of the Israelite experience when they were in the Tabernacle and Temple. It was not the building that experienced God's Glory but the people in it!

Today the church is looked upon as the building, but Paul talks of US AS THE CHURCH, being part of Christ's Body. (Eph. ch.4v12). It is the institutional church which has to understand this. It needs revelation and healing.

REFORMING THE CHURCH?

Today many in the UK are greatly in debt, the Government is also in serious debt; we are practically bankrupt. What can we do? How about following the answer of those in the Second World War and praying? So, who do we pray to and what do we say? I have mentioned "The Lord's Prayer", which is a good place to start. Praying can be simply talking to God – as if you are talking to your dad or a friend. Sometimes a short panic prayer is all you can manage. In times of danger, "Help!" is a useful prayer to cry out as you near the edge of the precipice! When your mind is in turmoil, "Jesus help me!" will be sure to get an answer, even if you do not know Him.

There is much talk today of mental illness; depression, with people confined to their homes; and aggression due to being unable to meet friends or relatives and having no-one to share their frustrations with. Or people suddenly explode with a fit of anger at their wife, children, elderly parent – some then become filled with remorse. The TV helps, or talking to others by Zoom, but that is not the same as speaking to them face-to-face. There can be a feeling of inadequacy, rejection, being unloved, a lack of purpose.

Is that how you feel? Try the emergency prayer. Go for a walk and listen to the birds singing, smell the flowers, see the beauty of nature which God created, and enjoy the peace and beauty of your surroundings. Be aware that God created all this and gave us eyes to see and ears to hear so we could appreciate nature, because He loves to share His creation with us. That is often what we miss most, the love of another person that is genuine and honourable, a feeling of warmth and comfort that lifts your spirit. Jesus loves us like that. His is an everlasting love that does not let us down, or criticise, or poke fun at our expense. He says, "Come to Me, my child, and let Me hug you because I love you."

* * *

Are Christians in churches prepared to come alongside those who need mental and spiritual help to enable them to overcome their distress? To show what is most important – our attitudes to each other? As Jesus loves and respects us, so He wants us to love and respect each other. Do we love and respect our parents, teachers, nurses. and doctors? Are we kind to friends, or criticise and poke fun at them? Do we encourage them on social media or write hateful messages? You see, most of us say we are good law-abiding people so would not deserve punishment, yet Jesus said we should worship God, His heavenly Father, and love our neighbours as ourselves. Can we say "yes" to both these commands? That's why we are in such a terrible state today. There is a saying that love makes the world go round, but it has to be an all-embracing agape love that looks to help others and care for them. I know we do not always feel like doing that, especially if others do not want to reciprocate, but there is a way.

ASK JESUS TO HELP!

Who is this Jesus? Some describe Him as love beyond measure. Others refer to the Bible, God's inspired word to us where He is described as the SAVIOUR of the world and each one of us, keeping us from God's punishment of hell for our unbelief. The HEALER of physical, mental, or emotional sickness. The REDEEMER, because Jesus suffered the punishment we deserved, by being put to death on a cross so that our sins and evil deeds could be forgiven by God. The BAPTISER in water, so we can die to self and ask Jesus into our lives, then receive the baptism of the HOLY SPIRIT, who comes to help us love and care for others.

We need to say sorry to Jesus for having ignored or rejected Him, and ask Him now to come into our lives? In fact, sorry does not seem to be enough, when we think of how Jesus suffered physically, being beaten, his flesh flayed with sharp bones on the end of the whips. It is more likely we should ask Him for mercy at how we have rejected Him, and seek His forgiveness.

IN BUT NOT *OF* THE WORLD

Jesus returned to heaven, and as we ask Him into our lives, we will go to be with Him and have everlasting life. But is that all there is to being a Christian? Well, no. There is much more to it. Salvation is only just the beginning of our spiritual lives. We are told that we live IN the world but are not OF the world. We are here to shed the light of Jesus into the world, to share His love, joy, and peace with our friends and neighbours, to pray for the Government, Israel, and the persecuted church. Yet above all we are encouraged to learn more about God and even hear Him speaking to us, by reading the Bible, God's inspired book which tells us more about Himself, how He revealed Himself first to Adam, then Abraham, Moses, and later – through Jesus – to the rest of the world.

In all these matters, Jesus did this to make it possible for God to dwell on earth and live within us. By dying then rising from death by the power of God, Jesus was the final, perfect sacrifice, meaning that when we say to God we are sorry for our sins, we are forgiven. Imagine no longer having to carry around the evil thoughts and actions and feeling guilty. We need have no fear of death because in Jesus we have eternal life! Jesus will heal our sickness and disease, if we ask Him. There is so much talk about the Covid virus with many suffering from long-term illness. There are different views about the vaccine and whether it can damage your immune system (which God put within us) and cause other body problems. Jesus will heal these problems if we ask Him. Many have a fear of diseases, of catching them from others or passing them onto other people. But you can give your worries and fears to Jesus and He will help you to overcome them. This is all part of God's Glory which we can share in, if we allow Him to enter into our hearts and listen to His guidance.

Oh, that we had that same fear and awe of God today! We might be allowed to call Him Father, yet we forget

He is our Creator, Provider, Protector, and Mighty God!
We sing "to be in His presence", but do we really know
what that means? To have an awesome respect and
humility before God, recognising how dependant we are
on Him? Even the supposed global warming is in God's
control, and puny man can do little to change it! Getting
to know more of God is a lifetime learning experience.

* * *

BECOMING DISCIPLES – THE HOLY SPIRIT

We can get to know more of God through learning to
pray, alone or with others; reading the Bible, which is His
inspired word to us; meeting other Christians and sharing
the wonders of God, in prayer and praise; encouraging
each other when we have needs, and knowing God's peace
and joy within our hearts as our hurts and cares are lifted
from us.

Does this still seem to be a tremendous task to
undertake? It would be if we had to do it all alone, but on
His return to heaven Jesus sent His Spirit, the Holy Spirit,
to help us. The Holy Spirit teaches and empowers you.
He enables you to become more like Jesus. In his letter
to the Ephesians Paul talks about the "fruits of the Spirit"
and identifies them as "love, joy, peace, patience, kindness,
goodness, and self-control". (Gal. 5 v22). It is impossible
to adopt all those attributes without the help of the Holy
Spirit. Then we are given different gifts, by the Holy Spirit,
to help others. Gifts of healing, have God-given knowledge
and wisdom, be able to speak God's words prophetically,
or interpret what other say in tongues so other Christians
also hear from God (Rom.12v6-8). There is more to being
a Christian than attending church on a Sunday morning!

If you would like more of God's Holy Spirit power within you, ask Him. Then your spirit will become in tune with God's Spirit.

The Holy Spirit, being a Spirit, could be everywhere at once, with thousands and thousands of angels to do His bidding in helping and protecting us, standing against the enemy, the territorial demons, and so on. Paul tells us to pray when in difficulty, and for the wisdom of governments and those who are in authority. (1Tim. ch.2v1-2) The Holy Spirit can also help us when we are sick, depressed, or in financial difficulty – if we ask Him. You can do that by praying, which is why praying is so important.

CHAPTER ELEVEN

Empowering the church

I have already said that congregations are decreasing and churches closing. There needs to be a new Reformation in the land involving true Christians – the Ekklesia, who fear God and have kept faith with Him, in worship, prayer, and intercession, seeking His Glory and His presence, looking for His guidance and praying it into being. This is the real church that God is calling for today. So, as we pray "Your Kingdom come on earth", we will use the power and authority God has given us to bring it into existence. For we are the light of the world, with Jesus at our head.

Now, why did this virus remain, not going away as they usually do, like the flu virus? There are many answers that some would call conspiracy theories, but I do not intend to go into all that. I'd rather look at another aspect – not the physical one of sickness, being out of work, having no income, no food for the children, schools closed, coping with children and parents all living together under one roof for days, even weeks. Let us look instead at the spiritual aspect. After all, we are Christians, churchgoers, worshipping and praising God with hymns and prayers and social fellowship after the service. So, we must know something about things spiritual, mustn't we?

7 8

Yes! There is much more to being a Christian. Salvation is only just the beginning of our spiritual lives. We are told that we live IN the world but are not OF the world. We are here to shed the light of Jesus into the world, to share His love, joy, and peace with our friends and neighbours, to pray for the Government, Israel, and the persecuted church. Yet we are not expected to do this all alone. The Holy Spirit will empower the church, if we ask Him.

DISCIPLESHIP

I spent some time when describing how God revealed Himself to a Nation. How He gave specific instruction about the dimensions of the Tabernacle, then the Temple in which God would reside. He gave detailed instructions about the implements to be used and what they were to be made of – wood, metal, or stone – but especially the colours in the curtains, which had special significance. Then when completed, with the holy of Holies divided from the rest of the building, containing the "Ark of the Covenant", I related how God's Glory entered so powerfully that no-one else could enter. God knew it was important to remind the Israelites of His closeness to them. In the wilderness, when Moses went into the Tabernacle to commune with God, the people were aware that Moses was meeting with God's Presence, and they all stood up in reverence. In the Temple, when the priests were worshipping, praying, and making sacrifices to God, they were aware of His Glory and Presence within the Holy of Holies where the "Ark of the Covenant" resided. Is this what is missing in our times of worship? Do we need to seek the Lord for more of His Presence?

THOUGHTS OF OTHERS

Derek Prince gave a definition of glory as God's "visible, tangible presence made manifest to man's senses". Now I know we can see and appreciate God's presence all around us. It is good to walk my dogs in the local Mill Meadows, to hear the birds sing, trees wafting their branches in the breeze, and see the beautiful colours of the spring flowers, the greenness of the grass as Spring changes into summer, with the sun shining in a clear blue sky. This must be something of God's tangible presence which I can appreciate with my senses of sight and hearing, I thought. But when Derek Prince talks about God's Glory in the church, he also talks of the "personal presence of Almighty God and a church that has entered into a relationship with God, through faith, where His visible, personal, tangible presence is with His people". Is that what we as a church have in our midst now? Yes, the praise and worship are wonderful, prayers, preaching, maybe testimonies. Children singing, tea and cake afterwards. Is that all we can expect – or perhaps there is more?

My search for answers to this question continued. What is this tangible, personal presence of God that Derek Prince talks about? Is there a greater awareness of God to be experienced? I've asked a number of committed Christians about this, and they have admitted to having lacked this deeper experience in church, too.

Then the Lord led me to another book. The title is *Ten Levels of Glory*, and it was written by Hrvoje Sirovina. Is this the answer to my searching? The first five levels he describes were something of a disappointment. To come to know Jesus; ask Him into your life and become "born again"; water baptism, then baptism by the Holy Spirit; receive His gifts; and speak in tongues. But I've done all that, I thought! Chapter six was rather different and a challenge to me. God had asked Solomon what he would wish for; God then asked Hrvoje. He thought long and hard as this would be only one gift so he wanted it to be one that would help him to best advance the Kingdom of God to His Glory.

Hrvoje considered a number of things, like faith, peace, revelation, passion, or love, but wondered if any of these would be the best thing for advancing the Kingdom, so rejected each in turn. Then he read Ecclesiastes ch.12v13: "Fear God and keep His commandments, for this is man's all." To FEAR God. Not be afraid of Him but to have an awe of God, respect Him, in reverence and admiration. Do I have such a fear of God? I wondered. When we worship in a church meeting, with our singing, clapping, and dancing, do we do that with an awesome fear of God or are we enjoying ourselves and having a good time?

Is our desire to give God the Glory, to seek His presence and hear from Him with the Spiritual gifts? He has given us knowledge of tongues and Interpretation, words of knowledge, wisdom, and prophetic utterances to teach us more of Him, to know the way He is leading and even understand the way He want us to go and direct others? Should we be seeking God's guidance in this time of confusion? Or is the church to remain quietly on the sidelines, nodding serenely, knowing God is in control so letting Him get on with it? The Glory and presence of God has gradually receded as it did in Ezekiel's time. (ch.10v4) No longer do we hear a prophetic word to guide the Government and Church in times of trouble, or stand against the illegal closing of the churches, causing isolation and preventing the opportunity to praise and worship God together. No longer is the Holy Spirit invited into many churches to bring in God's Presence and Glory.

SPIRITUAL RATHER THAN
PHYSICAL INFLUENCE

My search for a real answer continued. Looking back again, it seemed that at the end of the Second World War people were happy it was over. They could relax, cope with a return to daily work with enough income to feed the family, have a house over their heads, and recover from the devastation of war. The many men who had been called up into the armed forces wanted to recover from whatever they had experienced when at war. Many women who had assisted in various activities, making war weapons, being back-up for men in the Fire Brigade, Air Force and so on, began to realise that they wanted more than just to return to being mothers raising families. They wanted to go out to work, have a career, earn their own money, and be more independent.

Church, for some, became a secondary priority. In the background others were at work with their own ideas. It so happened in 1950 that a law was passed in Parliament to make witchcraft legal. A new spirit was arising! Most Christians probably had no idea of the significance of this. True, during the war there had been prayers when the nation was in dire need, but all that was over. The Lord had answered, and we had won!

Underneath the search lights, so to speak, another plan was being made to change the spiritual nature, culture, and society of this nation. It could be summed up as:-

Ten-point plan to destroy Christianity

1. Take God and prayer out of the education system
2. Destroy parental authority over the children
3. Destroy the Judeo-Christian family structure

4. Make sex free and abortion legal
5. Make divorce easy and free people from the concept of marriage for life
6. Make homosexuality an alternative lifestyle
7. Debase art, make it run mad
8. Use media to promote a change of mindset
9. Create an interfaith movement
10. Get governments to make all these laws and get the church to endorse these changes

Over the succeeding years Parliament has passed laws which have run closely to these ten points. Abortion, divorce, alternative lifestyle, education, the media, interfaith – before our very eyes, these ten points have mysteriously been achieved. The church, still asleep, has not generally noticed. The thought that another spirit would rise up never crossed the minds of most Christians, yet Paul said in his letter to the Ephesians, ch.4v12, that we do not fight against flesh and blood but against principalities, against powers, against the rulers of the darkness of this age, against spiritual hosts of wickedness in the heavenly places.

Christians, let us wake up and learn to stand against these evil forces!

Yes, God has been shaking as He said He would, to stir us up to realise what has happened and do something about it. But what can we do? It is important to put God first, to acknowledge He is King of Kings and Lord of Lords over all that would try to pull us down. This is why I was so delighted when God caused me to look at His Shekinah Glory. The church has to look again at seeking God's glory, with the Holy Spirit pouring out His Spiritual

Presence to empower us and cause us to rise up to be the people God intended.

THE WAY FORWARD

There is another reason for my emphasising where the people of the church are at present. It will explain why we have fallen so far at this time, and how we can rise up again to do the work which God has created us to be – our destiny. Many believe the British Isles were mentioned as long ago as the book of Genesis ch.10v5: "from these the coastland peoples of the Gentiles were separated into their lands". Isaiah ch.41v1 and v 5: "Keep silent before Me, O coastlands" … "The coastlands saw it and feared." Another Bible version (NIV) calls the coastlands "Distant Isles". Coastlands are also mentioned in Ezekiel ch.26v15. In ch.60v9, it says: "Surely the coastlands will wait for Me." And in the same verse says: "and the ships of Tarshish will come first". Ez. ch.27v12: "Tarshish was your merchant … They gave you silver, iron, tin." And verse 25 says: "The ships of Tarshish were carriers of your merchandise." It is thought by some scholars that Tarshish refers to Cornwall. From there, merchants went to Jerusalem to provide metals for Solomon's temple.

God has used the British Isles before to reach out to other nations with the Gospel message. When sailors began to sail across the oceans, they took the Christian way with them, and in the nineteenth century Christians went as missionaries across much of the world. Wherever they took possession of the land – India, Africa, China, and beyond – the gospel message was spoken. This continued to some extent well into the twentieth century. But although the UK was instrumental in naming Palestine as the land to be the home of the Jews, with the Balfour Declaration of 1917, when it came to being a reality, the UK Government tried to stop it. God immediately took away our Empire! And we have been floundering ever since.

Yet we are still called by God to fulfil our destiny, to be missionaries for Jesus across the world. However, it does not seem possible that we will ever again be fit to reach out to other nations when we are at war and encouraging arms to be sent to Ukraine for rather dubious reasons. But God can change things, draw us back to Him, and enable us to be obedient again to His calling.

NEED THE EKKLESIA TO STAND AGAINST THE ENEMY

I was led recently to Hosea ch.6v1. Hosea was talking to the people of Israel who had rebelled against God and rejected His Laws. "Come let us return to the Lord." And verse 2: "After two days He will revive us; on the third day He will raise us up." If there is to be a Reformation of the church, we need to start with ourselves. Having read again the "Ten points to destroy Christianity", I noted with dismay that each box could be ticked, and it happened under my nose without me noticing. Lord, forgive me for sleeping my time away, not standing against the enemy.

The church stood by without a murmur; in fact, some leaders agreed with many points and did not try to protest. I am reminded of what Jesus said to the church of the Laodiceans. "I know your work, that you are neither cold nor hot… because you are lukewarm, and neither cold nor hot, I will spew you out of My mouth." Lord, I am so sorry that I've been lukewarm. Stir me up with your refiner fire. You say that because You love me, You rebuke me, but then You stand at the door and knock. Help me to hear You and respond that I might be an overcomer.

Where the established church is lukewarm, Lord, may You call out those who are also repenting – the Ekklesia, the true church. Help them to also listen and respond to Your voice and be overcomers. May we seek Your Holy Spirit to lead us to Your Shekinah glory, where we may be empowered, anointed, and prepared to stand against the enemy. Would You raise up Elijahs, prepared like him, to demonstrate the power of God. May there be those You anoint to be Apostles, planting new works, Prophets hearing what You are saying to the Ekklesia, Evangelists spreading the Gospel, Pastors to be Shepherds to the flock, and Teachers explaining the scriptures to disciples.

We desperately need anointed leaders speaking Your prophetic words to the community, particularly to secular leaders. Lord, You say we should pray for the government, and we ask that You will bless them with Your wisdom and discernment. Guide them that they may know your way and go forward with Your power. Show us all of the Ekklesia how to stand against the powers and principalities of darkness that we might pull down the evil work of the enemy, so schools will no longer teach extreme sex to young children, parents will have full authority over their offspring, abortion will cease, and the media will promote what is good, kind, and honest. This nation will return to the Judeo-Christian principles, doing as Jesus, loving our neighbour as ourselves. Lord, would You cause the Ekklesia to change this nation back to You, that we might be ready again to acknowledge the heritage with which you blessed us, and the Kingdom purposes You have ordained for us. In Jesus' name.

A FRESH START?

After Abraham died, his son Isaac was told by God to stay in the land of the Philistines. But as Isaac was blessed by

God, he became prosperous and there were problems. The Philistines became jealous and blocked up all the wells that Abraham had dug, and which Isaac's cattle would drink from. Abimelech, King of the Philistines, told Isaac to move away so Isaac moved and his servants dug new wells, but the Philistine herdsmen quarrelled with Isaac's herdsmen and he had to move again. The same happened with the next well his servants dug, and Isaac moved on again to another place, and this time there was no quarrelling when the well was dug. (Gen. ch.26v22) Isaac had a fresh start, and there was peace.

So with the church today. There are disagreements, breakaways, different interpretations of scripture, and Christians looking for peace, moving away from their church or out of church completely. It is time to look for new wells to dig which bring us back to God, His blessings, and His leading. Amos prophesied that God would bring the exiles back to Jerusalem, saying, "On that day I will raise up the Tabernacle of David which has fallen down and repair its damages. I will raise up its ruins and rebuild it as in the days of old." (Amos ch.9v11) I believe this is what God wants to do in these "distant Isles". First, we need to heed the words of Hosea. "Come let us return to the Lord, for He has torn us but He will heal us." (Hos. ch.6v1)

Church, the Ekklesia is called to rise up and shine, stand against the enemy, by declaring God's will and His way! There is a kind of stirring in the church today, to seek God for revival, but I believe God is saying first we need to repent and be obedient to His commands. Not to kill (abortion), to honour God's plan for husband (male) and wife (female) to come together and create a family which He can bless. To come to know God as He is – awesome, powerful, almighty, the living God –and to come to know even more of Him by reading His words in the scriptures, to hear His plans for us and the way forward.

We are called to be the prophetic guide to Government and especially pray for protection of the children and families, that God will bring peace and protection so children can grow up in security, knowing they are loved and have a purpose in life, as does this nation. God gave warnings in the 1980s. One in particular was when the new Bishop of York was installed, who did not believe the Bible was God's revealed word for today. A lightning bolt came from a clear blue sky and hit York Minster, causing severe damage. More recently St Martin's in London burst into flames and was nearly destroyed. The vicar had said recently she was sorry that same sex marriage could not take place and apologised to the LBGT community for this. But God's word is specific about this. God loves all His creation and expects us to do the same, but that does not mean His word is to be ignored.

God's words are powerful but not to be changed (Rev. ch.22v18 &19). The Bible is as relevant today as when it was written, and we are to use it as we work with God. He could do it all alone but has chosen to work with us to overcome the enemy. It is important that we do His bidding, so we need to seek God for His way, be like the men of the tribe of Issachar, and know the times and the way to go. There are many Christians in the UK, the Ekklesia, who know the times – both the physical and the spiritual – but are we as clear about the way to go?

Then the Lord brought me to read another book entitled *Turnaround Covenant* – a way to be positive on the attack against the enemy. Some may stop here and think this is too much, but Jesus said to those who believe that He has given the power and authority to cast out demons. (Mk. ch.16v17)

The way is to stand on the covenant of God. When I was telling you of how God revealed Himself to one man, then a nation, He confirmed His revelations by speaking a COVENANT, which grew in content as He revealed more of Himself. Remember, the covenant was confirmed by the shedding of blood, the life of all creatures. To the Jews in the Old Testament, there were many rules and conditions. With the death of Jesus, the shedding of His Blood, and His resurrection, there was a NEW COVENANT. God knew sinful humans could never not commit sins. But through Jesus we could repent and be forgiven, so Satan the enemy could be overcome, by using the words of God's covenant to us in declaring and decreeing, binding and loosening.

So, to use one of the decrees from *Your Nation Needs YOU* by Jill Gower and the "House of Prayer" in Norwich: "We Declare and Decree that the Lord has not finished with this nation" yet. If we are the "Distant Isles" (Is. ch.49v1) Isaiah spoke of, then we have more work to do, but first the nation has to be spiritually cleansed before we are fit to reach out again to other countries with the Gospel message. Repentance and calling on God for His mercy is essential, but also reminding Him of His covenant to us – that He loves us, heals us, delivers us from evil, and empowers us through His holy Spirit. He will protect us, guide us, and lead us in ways of righteousness, will come close to us with His Presence, His Shekinah Glory. A covenant which gives us an identity: we belong to Jesus, we will be restored as a church, a family, and as a nation.

God's covenant stands against the covenants of the enemy. Those Ten points I mentioned clearly state what the enemy has done. Now it is for us, with God's help, to pull down what has been put up against God and the Ekklesia. We have such a great and mighty God, full of compassion and love, with a plan that is not yet complete. The calling to the British Isles is to overcome the enemy, to reveal Jesus to the world, and in fact to become a Covenant Nation again. I pray, Lord Jesus, that Your Holy Spirit will blow on the UK as Ezekiel did to the dry bones of Israel, that we may again rise up and live! Glory to God! Amen.

And Finally...

I thought I'd finished, until the Lord caused me to look again this book *Turnaround Decrees*, by Jon and Jolene Hamill, about a group of American Christians who have been meeting to seek the Lord for prophetic direction. Jon and Jolene Hamill have described how they were led to pray for a turnaround, as they believe the Lord is wanting Christians in America to see from scriptures how the situation is so evil in the US – and, I might add, in the British Isles – and that God is encouraging them to pray for a complete change, back to righteousness, honesty, purity, and holiness. The pulling down of all that is evil in the schools, Government, finance, etc., things which are spiritual as well as physical, and to be led by the Lord Jesus to search scriptures for decrees which will cause this "turnaround". You will have to read the book to find out more, but this is the challenge the Lord has given me, and hopefully you, too. To seek God for His guidance in finding decrees for this nation, which He will honour, to cause the British Isles to be prepared and ready to be the Nation which God intended us to be, purposed to tell the world about Jesus and influence cultures to be more like His ways.

So, rise up, oh Church, hear the words of the Lord. Go forth in the power of the Holy Spirit to pull down the strong holds binding the nation. Pray that the Lord will cause us to turn around, back to the ways of God, that the Temple might be repaired, and the Shekinah Glory of the Lord be revealed, so we will again worship and praise His glorious Name!

Susan McCaffery

Milton Keynes UK
Ingram Content Group UK Ltd.
UKHW040846050124
435493UK00005B/569